CLIMBING
the
GLASS
MOUNTAIN

A Father's Amazing Journey into Spirituality

ALLEN AND DAVID
GLINIEWICZ

Climbing the Glass Mountain
Copyright © 2023 David Gliniewicz

Edited and Formatted by The Book Khaleesi

TABLE of CONTENTS

DEDICATION

Thanks to my dad, for taking me on such an amazing journey, and so many other gifts.

Thanks to all my family for the inspirations that sparked and shaped these pages.

I am grateful to Eeva Lancaster for her support, brilliant suggestions, and editing, for this, my first book.

My wife Ellen and William Ward for their excitement and energy given when I first pitched the idea of this book, Ellen too for that spark when first listening to my original draft.

To my children Grace and Finn, whom I see as truly inspiring with their accomplishments, these fill me with love and pride!

Lexi, I have appreciation for you showing me who you are and for giving me such inspiration, you are stricken with the mind of an engineer, and your spirit is so much in these pages.

Joseph for saving my inner life and heart, and for allowing me to see my dad for who he is. Additionally, I have an enormous amount of gratitude for Dr. Jonathan Cohen for his support, inspiration, and encouragement of the Gliniewicz family for decades, which now culminates in these pages.

For the original impetus to create a memoir for Allen, from Leah Betancourt. Leah first pitched the idea while visiting Allen. Leah and Al's ensuing discussion about the memoir, was enough to get the wheels turning, and was the seed for the creation of this book.

Also, to Dr. Patricia Coughlin for clearing the way for the completion of this memoir and healing myself, and my family! Without your help this work would not have been possible.

This book is a result of your energy given freely to me, bless you all!

FORWARD

David Gliniewicz, Allen's son, asked me if I would write something to accompany the book that he is editing and co-writing with his father, and I am honored to contribute.

I have known Allen for close to forty years. My feelings about Allen have ranged from being overwhelmed by his intellect and fire, as I first knew him, to recently a deep, warm awe of this being who is called Allen Gliniewicz.

I have always known him to be a Renaissance man, so it both delighted and did not surprise me that he was inspired by an artist of the period. Allen is a true "spelunker" who will go digging into finding truth at most any cost. He is an effective miner, as his intellect is incredibly strong. As the years have moved along, so has his spiritual deepening, so as an octogenarian, his ability to perceive has deepened.

Albert Einstein said, "Everyone who is seriously involved in the pursuit of science, becomes convinced that a spirit is manifest in the laws of the Universe – a spirit vastly superior to that of man, and one in the face of which we with our modest powers must feel humble." Allen lives in that awe and humility.

If you did not know his combination of brilliances, you might think him mad, as his explanations of things are informed by not only the intellect, but also contact that he has from beyond. When I first met him, my mind and capacity to think about things was "boundaried" by the here and now. As a result, I saw Allen's thinking and musing as an irritant and wished he would deal with the "here and now" more. As I have deepened and expanded spiritually, I have been better able to appreciate his brilliance. But even more than appreciating his intellectual gifts, I have been able to appreciate his intention. His deepest intention is to create healing on our planet.

As a man close to ninety years old, he is completely committed to finishing his memoirs to inform us about how the world works both materially and spiritually. Allen acts as a guide and indicates to us that which we can do to heal the planet and ourselves.

Despite a multitude of medical infirmities, he uses most of his waking hours to complete this incredible tome. His son David, who has been inspired by his father, has been devoted to compiling, editing, transcribing, and offering commentary for the work of Allen Gliniewicz.

– **Dr. Jonathan Cohen**

AUTHOR'S NOTE

The views expressed in this book are unconventional and are not being shared in promotion of any spiritual view. Polytheism is a subject that does come up, though it is presented as an anecdote only. My own personal spiritual views are not represented in these pages. I leave it to each reader to know that their spiritual views are their own and neither Allen nor I have any right to impose spiritual views on anyone. This book is an exploration of my father's life and experiences, and I can't tell this story without mentioning the spiritual realm.

– David Gliniewicz

Me, with my Dad, Allen

Before We Begin

Thank you for sharing this journey with my father and me! In this volume, I am attempting to tell the story of Allen Gliniewicz and to let his voice be as true as possible throughout our time together.

I will make commentary if I feel there needs to be some context or to make things clearer, because we may go to some unlikely places in these pages.

Allen worked in technical fields at major aerospace and technology companies throughout his unusual life.

During this multifaceted career, which includes work with NASA, and nearly all the Apollo missions, Allen most notably worked on Apollo 11 and Apollo 13.

My dad also had a spiritual life which drove many of his actions and accomplishments. I will include direct quotes to channel my dad's voice as faithfully as possible.

In part one of our journey, The Mundane World, encompassing the first six chapters of this book, my dad's story was steeped in this mundane world we happen to share. Allen dealt with absolutes here, such as crises at NASA with Apollo 13, and providing for a large family at the same time.

When the veil of everyday existence was later pulled from Al's eyes, a new, larger world was revealed. This new dimension was one where the spirit world was not an abstract, a world where messages come from the spirit realm, and God.

These experiences, however, did not fit so neatly into the world in which my dad had mastered his place so well, and there was resistance to my dad's new experiences, both from within himself and from those around him.

In the state of mind which the mundane world creates in us, one in which our minds are cemented in the confines of the accepted paradigm, reality is then fixed – in our view – and there is no further room for any change.

To better bring an understanding of the dimensions and workings of our world, we can choose a patron saint who can symbolize the entirety of the mundane world. Someone who showed the absolute best this world has to offer during their life, in terms of both artistic expression and scientific innovation.

Leonardo DaVinci, *the* artist of the Renaissance, was a truly significant person in his time on Earth, and a person who perhaps sums up our mundane world entirely.

DaVinci's *Vitruvian Man*– the diagram of the human body, drawn in its symmetry – was chosen as the symbol to represent Earth on the Pioneer plaques. These plaques, which grace the hulls of the spacecraft Voyager 1 and 2, provide, in their symbols, the sum of human existence in a concise and compact form. These plaques represent our highest achievements and our *essence* to any alien race, in an anticipated, possible chance encounter, as the craft go farther into the void of space than we have ever previously reached.

The Renaissance was a period responsible for uplifting humanity from the Dark Ages. DaVinci was at the forefront of the Renaissance, with his contributions to science, and his inventions – the armored tank, propeller, and models of winged flight – and, perhaps most recognizably, with his celebrated *Mona Lisa*.

My father loved DaVinci and had an enormous volume with all his works. As a child, I would page through this huge book. I could not say this as a child, but something, for me, was ultimately unsatisfying about DaVinci's work, perhaps because it dealt *entirely* with the mundane world.

His designs for implements of war – for instance, the tank – are the fruits of a mind solving issues for our mundane world, similar to the way my dad contributed to the Minuteman missile and the Apollo missions. Except for the *Mona Lisa's* smile, DaVinci's work, though amazingly beautiful, is without mystery. This was something that bugged me about DaVinci, though I didn't know exactly why it did at the time.

Another artist, Salvador Dali, whom Al also loved, could be the patron saint for part two of this book, The Ethereal Summit. Dali was the opposite of DaVinci, and brought another dimension to his work, that of the ephemeral world, the one we see and explore in dreams.

My dad's original title for his memoir was *The Patching of Our Universe / Climbing the Glass Mountain*. This title was forged in the mundane world and like DaVinci's work, a facet of reality was perhaps lost.

Though my dad was spiritually attuned, he was still in the box of traditional, worldly roles for most of his life.

To sum up my dad's experience, we can say he had a more docile ear attuned to the spiritual than he now has, and this has created some change.

Part two, *Through the Looking Glass*, is the destination for the overarching story of my father's journey, one of becoming a new being. This new world, beyond the small concerns of the mundane, is a reinvented existence which wrestles with larger questions and knowing the seemingly unknowable.

The etheric plane, in which I feel Allen now largely lives in his mind, is not without significant dangers, however. In this new environment in the ether, hostile entities are common, and can take advantage of those who are unprotected.

Later in our journey together, we will explore the spiritual, other-worldly journey Allen took. However, to demonstrate the caution and preparation needed for such a journey, our discussion here will also be a cautionary tale, as this journey cannot be taken lightly.

Why do climbers die on Mount Everest, and sherpas largely survive such a monumental climb?

Perhaps, the reason is that modern climbers are increasingly chasing the summit of Everest for worldly reasons. A reason for a westerner to climb Everest might be getting an adrenaline rush, or bragging rights – all trademarks of our mundane world, like DaVinci thinking that all things can be overcome with technology.

As an example of our faith in technology, the Concord could fly from New York to London in just under three hours, and it was thought that the atomic bomb could end all war.

We can believe that there is a magic, technological bullet for each situation and problem. We, unfortunately, believe we've tamed nature and have lost our respect for and perhaps our reverence for our creator. Sherpas have a vastly different reason for reaching the summit of Everest – to them it's a spiritual journey, and this may be why they are vastly more successful in doing it.

The book and film *Into Thin Air*, by Jon Krakauer, is a perfect example of the lack of reverence in our tech-heavy world. We expect safe adventures, where the danger is filtered out, so that there are only benefits in the activity, without any of the risks. This is the expectation of a modern climber of Everest, to jet over on a weekend and get back to the daily grind at work at the end of the journey, and with stories to tell at the watercooler.

And perhaps to a sherpa, Everest is a symbol of attainment with the divine, and that a personal struggle is required to reach the top. Another requirement of the sherpas could be gaining purity and dropping all spiritual baggage as a part of the journey to the physical summit. Through purification, a personal summit is reached inside the heart of a sherpa. The physical summit is just the outward appearance of an inward journey. A deep respect of the mountain is within the heart of the sherpa, where any physical test is merely a test of faith in God to allow obstacles to be removed from within and without simultaneously.

So, if we are invited to explore a spiritual realm, do we do it with our mundane mind or the heart of a sherpa? This question of how attuned we are to the divine is one that may determine the outcome and reveal the amount of our resolve and devotion, and seal our fate, for the summit is unforgiving.

Just as climbing a mountain is a challenge, we also find people and situations that either help or hinder our path in everyday life.

An example of our need to be cautious in our daily lives could be when we are dealing with people who have influence over us. There are some people we might need to distance ourselves from to be our best, and some people whose advice we should take, while there are some we should not.

It is even more important to be discerning when dealing in the world of dreams and symbols and spirits. It can be harder to see the pitfalls and harder still to undo falling into one.

Just like leveling up in a video game, a higher plane of existence brings with it higher stakes and more risk of catastrophe.

This part of our journey with my dad will touch on the ethereal realms and it will be unfamiliar ground for us. We see Al as he is learning to cope with losing some abilities while gaining others and grappling with his new role in a shifted and shifting context of finding himself in an uncharted and malleable, outland territory.

Allen is like an astronaut, or perhaps Captain Kirk, boldly going where no man has gone before. I don't think our "Kirk" will be making out with any green aliens on our journey, though.

Some might say it's senility, what Allen experiences

now, or a compromise of his mental processes.

I have had unconventional spiritual experiences myself, and I'm possibly the best one, the most able to see my dad exactly where he is now, in all its magnificence. The world in which my dad now lives is an amazing and unlimited place. I'm happy that I'm able to share my dad's experiences through my relationship with him during the changes he has experienced and share them with you here.

In a few ways, we can compare my dad's story to that of Ram Dass, formally Richard Alpert. Ram Dass too was from the mundane world, and a success as a Harvard professor. Through transcendent experiences, Ram Dass was able to break out of the box of the "normal" gestalt in the world of academia.

As a result of no longer fitting into the traditional role of a Harvard professor, the academic community banished Ram Dass, whom they saw as a crazy person, and no longer part of the rational world, in which we supposedly live.

"The question is, do we allow the moment to be real or not?"

– Ram Dass, Conscious Aging

Do we allow my father to be who he is now? Does he allow himself to be his new, larger self? Or do we label Allen, and in doing so, separate from him?

Let me say that no one is an island and that who we

allow people to be ultimately makes a difference to our loved ones, and what they might achieve. In giving our generous allowance to free others from the confines of our limiting feelings and attitudes, we play an enormous part in the personal freedom that our loved one can then allow themselves to experience.

I know that my dad is still with us. I also know he's changed, with a fundamental spiritual and cognitive shift.

As I hinted in my description of part one above, Salvador Dali was also loved by Allen, and another enormous volume of Dali's work graced the coffee table in our home.

Dali at first repulsed me with his sometimes disturbing and evocative imagery. However, Dali also scratched an itch in me that DaVinci did not, in speaking of the unconscious.

Dali, in his images, spoke of an amorphous world in which possibilities and potentials were hidden within a veil. When the observer stepped over a threshold of understanding, the veil lifted and the secret was revealed, showing the previously subliminal and otherworldly message. Surprises lurking beneath the surface of images could either leap on us and bring on an "ah-ha" moment, or, through a slower process of visual double entendre, these would gently slide into our awareness, with little or no notice by us at all that anything had happened.

Dali's ability to bring a metaphysical dimension to his work is closely tied to Freud and Carl Jung's symbolic archetypes. These hold an extra-dimensional power and bring a new aspect to my dad's story.

Dali was the shadowy counterpart to DaVinci's sobriety, illustrating a dimension of which we were not yet aware.

As Al became further steeped in an alternative reality, he wanted, of course, to share what he had learned and experienced with me and with the world.

In this book, I believe I have helped to create the right vehicle for passing on all the insights and experiences my dad wants to share.

From our perspective, it's not at all easy for us to accept a new reality. We invest a lot of time and effort to grasp what we think the world is and we are often uncomfortable with anything that might upset our ideas.

Another thing my dad has is a sense of individuality. He doesn't care too much about what others may think. I feel I've both benefitted from and been hurt by this belief, which I inherited from him.

Others have had the same struggle of non-acceptance when trying to share a radically different perspective. Ever since Prometheus stole fire from the gods, it's been an issue to explain the unexplainable!

It's human nature to resist change. At least maybe at first, we often need to go through a process to accept new information that may challenge us and shatter our carefully constructed ideas.

I feel there was such an enormous resistance to allowing Ram Dass to be his new self after he gained insight from his experiences in a reality outside our usual one. This resistance, no doubt, which removed Ram Dass from the Harvard faculty, was born out of fear, as is always the case in shutting down someone who challenges us. It serves to keep us comfortable.

Incidentally, Ram Dass was able to overcome the resistance and to avoid getting stuck in our cultural models through the incredible amount of traveling he did. This took Ram Dass out of his environment and side-stepped all the cultural rigidity that we have. In his travels, Ram Dass found liberation, and if there is anything to shatter cultural barriers, it's travel!

I guess this is why there is a practice of renaming in India, when an individual begins a spiritual journey. The new name gives the individual space to expand, and the seeker is reborn and reframed spiritually. Through all the network of people who surround the now renamed seeker, this reframing of the individual allows a new becoming, a new person is born at this moment, the individual is new to themselves as well as the group, and the dormant potentiality is then unlocked.

Perhaps my dad needs a new name as well, to then allow him to reframe himself, a name in which the confines of this contracted world fall away, and the tether is removed. Our tether to Allen's heart might have a chance to fall away as well. This renaming and reframing is something that could be useful for us to loosen our chains, which have become so comfortable to us.

Let's see if we can allow the moment to be real or not. What a quiet revolution that could be!

PART 1:

The Mundane World

Prologue

David: I'm going to allow my dad to use his original, combined title in the prologue. It lends itself to telling his unique story, and even though the actual title of the book has evolved beyond this one, it sheds light on my dad's thoughts and personal journey, from where it started. This is where we join him.

Allen

I'm going to use Patching the Universe / Climbing the Glass Mountain. I use this combined title because it shows how the two points of view, the point of view of God and my own point of view, which together create my story. God has shown himself in my life and story through dreams and synchronicities and by placing me in the right places at the right times. This is how He is patching the universe. My actions and reactions to the visions and inspirations have shown how I'm climbing the glass mountain.

What I saw in my life, and how I used symbolic and dream imagery to guide me, is described in motif in *The*

CLIMBING THE GLASS MOUNTAIN

Yellow Fairy Book, in the tale, "The Glass Mountain." This story shows a sort of symbolic template of my life.

I will summarize this Polish story…

There was a glass mountain on which grew a tree with golden apples. One of these apples would grant the one who picked it access to the golden castle where a princess lived. Many knights had tried to climb the glass mountain, and the bodies of the brave failures littered the ground in the surrounding area.

A knight in golden armor tried and made it halfway up the mountain. He gave up when his horse slipped on the steep incline. The next day, he tried again and was attacked by an eagle. This caused the death of the knight and his horse, adding to the litter of spent knights at the halfway point to the summit.

A young student killed a mountain lion and used the animal's claws, which he repurposed as climbing gear for his own hands and feet. These gave him purchase and prevented his fall during his harrowing climb.

As the boy rested on the slope, tired from the grueling ascent, he spied an eagle looking for carrion. The boy lay near the body of the golden knight and pretended to be dead. The eagle carried the boy off, thinking he was a corpse. The eagle dug its claws into the boy. As it carried him to the top of the mountain, the boy suddenly cut off the eagle's feet to allow his escape.

The eagle lost its claws to the boy, and the boy fell into the golden apple tree. The peels of the apples cured his many wounds. The boy, having attained the summit, then married the princess.

The blood of the injured eagle was healing to all the knights who had perished in their attempt to climb the mountain. The eagle's blood brought them back to life.

David

I believe my father makes this comparison between the events of "The Glass Mountain" and his own life for these reasons.

Allen has always searched for the meaning of things, including the symbolic meaning of events and dreams.

My dad has allowed dreams and images from meditations to guide his decisions in the world throughout his life.

Through dream interpretation, Al has been able to work through challenges, similar to how the boy used the tools of the mountain lion's claws and the blood of the eagle to surmount seemingly impossible tasks. Through a partnership with the unconscious mind and dream symbology, my dad was able to channel the solutions to complex problems.

The sections of this book are broken up into the areas where Allen and the rest of the family lived. My dad provides his own personal observations and commentary, along with significant technology and career events. My father's work on the Apollo missions is one that is most interesting personally, and one that I see involving both incredible synchronicity and historical significance.

Regarding my dad's use of unconscious or dream imagery and his way of stating things only once in his story, he had this to say.

Allen

I try to make every effort, wherever I encounter imagery – from whatever source it may be, dreams, meditations, or other encounters – to present these images exactly the way they occurred, so that if someone doesn't agree with my interpretation, the raw data is there to maybe facilitate someone with greater depth and understanding than I have, or another opinion that may reflect, add to, or shed a different light on the symbol.

I'll try to describe significant visions and dreams only once, so that there will not be any artificial differences in saying things more than one way. In this way, I'll try to make it as clear as I can, to help the reader to understand the material in their own way as it first occurs to them. This could also help readers to reduce the volume of the material that they go through.

Chicago

Allen

Chicago is where I was born in 1935, in June. We lived in a Polish area. There was one incident that occurred that almost made a quick end to my life story.

My father had just come back from taking me for a long walk in a buggy when I was less than a year old. He brought me up to the door of the house where we were staying. He unlocked the harness from around me, but I just wouldn't sit down. He turned to unlock the door. When he turned back, I was already falling toward the pavement. And thank God for his quick reaction. He caught me by my diaper before I met the pavement. The unfolding scene was so shocking that two girls walking by screamed when they saw this from across the street.

So, you can say, my first flight into space was a success. [*Laughs.*] It almost ended right there.

Later, when I started school, was the first time that I'd encountered a lot of other children from different places, and I had a miserable time through that first year.

I had almost every childhood disease that there was. I was sick all but just a few weeks of the time. And, when I finally finished up, I had a severe case of scarlet fever just before I was seven years old, and it settled into an ear infection as well.

In the 1930s, antibiotic use was not common for the treatment of ear infections. This forced me into quarantine and, except for the candy store which my parents owned, me and my mother were quarantined at our place for several weeks.

We had to close it, of course. I was so ill. My mother was with me, and I was deeply thankful to her for taking care of me with minimal equipment, medical knowledge, or any help.

I just floated in and out of consciousness all during this time. She said my temperature went up to 106 degrees. I only remember a few hours of time during this period, but it left me with a sensitivity to any cold wind across both of my ears. I had this sensitivity for the next seven years, until I was fourteen years old. I finally grew out of it, but I just had to live with it every winter and fall until it eventually went away. I remember the pain would be so great that I felt like tearing off my ears, but I knew that wouldn't stop the pain. Sometimes the earaches hit both ears on the same night. This condition, I think, forced me to compensate by digging more deeply into myself. And I think that it really changed my personality.

I was told about the significance of these painful events and my ability to overcome them – this was by a psychologist, much later in my life – and I believe it's true!

And so, I became [*laughs*] the person I am.

I started school, and it wasn't long after that, before I was eight years old – this was 1943 – that my dad got drafted into the navy in World War II, and just before Easter, he had to go off to war, and left basically my mother and I to take care of the store.

David

It's worth noting that Stanley "Steve" Gliniewicz, my dad's father, went on to fight in the battle of Iwo Jima. During a particularly harrowing part of the battle, my grandfather promised God that if he made it through the battle, then he would go to church each Sunday for the rest of his life. God made good on that promise! Steve survived the battle. Steve also kept his part of the bargain and, wherever he went, he would attend church every Sunday. This powerful story of my grandfather, who then shared the subtle, yet influential, story with my dad, made an impression and stuck with Allen, as well.

To my dad, it was a powerful example of God affecting change in his father, Steve's, life. I believe it made an indelible impression on him that our choices and our alliances with higher powers can have beneficial effects. Also, there is evidence in my dad's early understanding that there is two-way communication and exchange from the mortal realm to the divine.

Allen

My mother taught me how to make change in the cash register. So, I would take care of the store when she was too tired to do it herself. She would get so tired that she would often sleep for a while. I ended up having what felt like unbelievable amounts of cash coming in from all my sales and uncountable numbers of errands – all kinds of things, like getting ice, newspapers, and postage stamps for the customers.

During this period, eventually, my mother just couldn't take working in the store by herself anymore, even with me helping as much as I could. We then arranged for my dad's younger brother and his wife to take over the store's operation until my dad came back from the service. As a result of no longer running the store, which was part of the house in which we were living, we had to move and go live in a different part of the city until my dad got back from the war.

Moving, of course, also meant switching school districts for both my sister and me. My sister was able to go to a parochial school which happened to be almost across the street from us at the new house in which we were living. But my dad – he wanted me to go to a different public school because he didn't want me learning Polish brogue from the sisters who taught at the school I would have been in. He thought it might perhaps prevent me from getting a job in the future.

So, I had to walk to a different school. [*Laughs.*] Then I walked into a whole nest of other problems. Here I was in fifth grade, and the school that I was assigned to had been destroyed by fire. So, they distributed the students among the neighboring districts. I had to walk across to a district on the other side of town. The children there were not friendly toward newcomers. The classes were already crowded prior to us coming there, and when we moved in, it forced the classes to overflow into the basement. And it led to fights at recess time. My sister Carol and I got beaten up regularly. The reaction of the teachers to the escalation in fights happening among the newcomers was to keep everybody busy. They just quadrupled the workload. They taught us all the next subjects up to and including eighth grade. As a result, I learned all the multiplication tables and the names of all the states and the capitals, also how to spell them, among a lot of other things. I even took piano lessons during this period – to keep me busy, so to speak. When my dad came back from the service, when the war was over, and we went back to our actual home and the store, I also went back into my regular school.

Everything was review for me at this point because I had been given such an accelerated curriculum to keep me busy at the other school and had learned years more material, so I had a great advantage. So [*laughs*] I got very good grades. I got a good head start, let's put it that way, better than most kids.

Then, in high school, I went to the inner-city school for a year, and we bought a new house right at the edge of the city, on the northwest side of Chicago, and I changed schools. I finished the last three years out there, and then eventually started at the University of Illinois.

Since it was a state-supported school in the city, I attended for two years at the navy pier where the school was located. Later, I went downstate for further studies after the foundational first years.

While studying downstate, I really wasn't satisfied with my progress. I had changed my major from engineering physics to physical chemistry. It was a struggle at the new location.

This really did me in [*laughs*] – I had to take an additional year of German instead of one. It was required to take two years. I could not learn the second year of German for some reason. The wall I hit in learning German forced me out of school for a while, but, worse than that, I lost my student deferment. This change in my status would make my life even more interesting shortly.

So, I went back to Chicago, and worked part-time as a chemist at the Pepsi-Cola bottling company, supervising the mixing of syrup and treatment of water that was required for making the drink. I started back in school after some time, only now I was going to the Illinois Institute of Technology, rather than the University of Illinois.

I performed well into my third year, but then at the end of this third year, the draft board caught up with me and inducted me into the army between my junior and senior years. [*Laughs.*]

I spent two years in the service in West Germany. Then I came back just in time to start senior-level physics. And that was a cute transition that woke me up a little bit, [*laughs*] but I did do very well. I was older and

12

more mature. As a matter of fact, I did manage to make the dean's list in that last year, although I was carrying extra classes to make up my credits for three different lab courses – atomic physics, electrical circuits, and optics.

With all these heavy labs, I was carrying eighteen credit hours – twelve hours during the day and six hours at night courses.

I managed to schedule a time so I could go over to see my girlfriend, Joan, whom I later married. I would see her on Thursdays, and it was a good way to relax, apart from studying.

I had no classes on this one day of the week, but I wouldn't go out unless I was all finished with my homework. And, by doing that, I somehow made the dean's list. It was a real surprise.

I eventually graduated from the Illinois Institute of Technology in 1961, in February. I was able to get my first job in engineering out of state, and we got ready to move from Chicago.

Seattle

Allen

These are the details of the trip out to Seattle.

I left Chicago with my wife, Joan, and I tried to get a weather forecast from the Chicago Motor Club, but they refused to give me anything, even if I bought a membership. [*Laughs.*] However, as I was walking out the door, I heard somebody yell from behind me that there was a snowstorm on the way, so that was my warning.

Well, we left, but before we got to St. Louis, which was about 250 miles away, there were five inches of snow on the ground. St. Louis is right at the corner of Missouri.

I had to cross a diagonally angled corner, and it was a solid sheet of ice. I had no chains with me, we were driving a Chevy – which was light in the back end – and the only way I could keep the car going straight ahead was to drive with two wheels in the shoulder's snow. This was so that the back end didn't start waving around behind us.

I was going as fast as I felt I could under those conditions. As we went along the frozen landscape, there were semi-trailer trucks off the long embankments, cracked up and disabled on both sides of the road.

So, we went along, and I've got Joan sitting up with me, five months pregnant, and all our worldly possessions packed in the car.

We then came over the crest of a hill and suddenly, about 300 yards ahead of us, there was an obstacle that was difficult and treacherous to avoid. A car had slid off the road, and a state trooper was there trying to help him. The level of danger was further amped up by the presence of these other idiot people who happened to be casually walking around on the road. I tried my best to slow down the car as much as I could, but I got caught in the tracks of snow and ice in the road and just slid down the embankment. I slowed and just barely got stopped just before it went over. We were within a foot and a half of the edge of a drop-off, which could have been the end of us.

It was that close. [*Makes a gesture with his hands about the size of a car steering wheel.*] I get out of the car and talk to the state trooper, who then courageously gets in front of our car, perched so near the drop-off, and starts to push. I'm in the back and pulling backward. Amazingly, after some hard effort, we backed out onto the road.

As we again struck back onto the treacherous road, I was trying to carefully avoid these – like I said, these idiot people who are wandering around the road. They were creating such a hazard for themselves and for others, they forced me to slow way down to carefully avoid them. I couldn't just run over those people. Right?!

That was the way we started, and we were creeping along the road and the hazards for the next I don't know how many miles. We went all the way to the other end of Missouri, and through just a little bit of Oklahoma, and I thought, well, we just must get some change in the weather, and this will be so much easier. It's just too dangerous to keep going the way we are. We are going to have to give up on this trip, in that case.

Soon, albeit briefly, I would get my wish.

We ended up going through the panhandle of Texas, through Amarillo. So, I stopped in Amarillo to buy some strap chains to put on. I get the chains and travel less than a half a mile, and suddenly, the temperature changes. The road is now *wet*. [*Laughs*.]

A little later, maybe only a few miles, we hit one of the worst sleet storms I've ever seen. The sleet was just forming an ice sheet over the car, and I had to keep on scraping off the air vents, so we could get enough air inside the car to circulate and keep the windows clear enough to be able to see where we were going.

In Texas, at that time at least, there were few road signs and no fences and very shallow culverts. When we were driving under these non-ideal conditions, we could not be sure that we were even on the road. We could have been out in the middle of the arroyo and would never have known. [*Laughs*.]

We came up, over a rise in the road, and there was a guy scraping frozen shards off his ice-sheathed car. The man was sitting in the middle of the road. He probably didn't even know that he was in the path of danger.

In the face of this latest obstacle, I'm fighting for control of the car, and I just happen to somehow go a bit around him, and then the car spins in a slow arc all the way around sideways and hits the man inexplicably gently, knocking him to the curb. And the guy, I did shake him up, but he was okay, we made sure he was all right.

He was desperate to get where he was going, though. He was struggling to see and stay on the road just like I was. He wanted to follow me, and I agreed to let him, to continue the way that I was going, so he'd know if he was on the road. So, we continue this way, and eventually he cuts off and goes in another direction. I guess he was confident on his own at that point.

Eventually, we come across the state of New Mexico, and I notice that the car is starting to handle a little funny. It's getting mushy, and as we come into Arizona, it's getting worse, growing softer, particularly on one side, and somehow squirrely, fishtailing sporadically.

I thought I'd pull over to the next gas station and find out what was going on with the steering and/or handling. What I do find is that there was only eighteen pounds of air in one of the back tires.

It turned out that when I did that spin around to avoid hitting the guy scraping his car in the middle of the road, it had torn the inside of the cord of the tire, and it was losing air. But you couldn't see it because it was on the inside of the tire. So, I had to buy a tire [laughs] right there, or that would be the end of the trip. After this, we continued on toward California, and Joanie said she wanted to visit the Grand Canyon. It's probably the only time in our lives where we'll be close enough to the canyon to go see it.

So, I acquiesce, and we drive ninety miles out of our way, straight up to the Grand Canyon, where you pull in and get a cabin at the Grand Canyon and Bright Angles Lodge. It's not a big cabin that they reserved for us, but it's beautiful, it's really an authentic frontier log cabin.

We pulled in there at night. And when we get up the next morning, we look out, we're less than 200 feet from the edge of the Grand Canyon. We could've walked out there in the dark, and there were no fences or walkways. We could have walked right out and fallen into that thing. It's a mile deep, and we had no idea how close we were to the end of the trip.

The next morning, we look at the beautiful Grand Canyon and thank God we're not at the bottom of it. And we went on our way. Again, we reached the state line between Arizona and California – Needles, California – and we stopped. They check us for fresh fruit… if we had any with us. Inspectors don't let you do that because they're worried about carrying insects across state lines.

My engine suddenly starts squeaking. It's squeaking like mad. And I didn't understand what was going on. I thought, *well, maybe the fan belt is loose and spinning, making a squealing sound.*

I ended up taking care of the squeal with a spray I happened to have with me. Cars were much less reliable then, as you can see from all the things that happened during this one trip. It just so happened that the spray was some sort of alcohol-based product, and I was spraying alcohol into a hot engine, but it did do the job and nothing more happened, at least for a time.

We start a seventy-eight-mile run from Barstow to the Mohave, with nothing in between. And as we're going to the Mojave, the engine, which I thought I'd fixed with the spray, is squeaking.

Oh, boy. I had all the fan belts replaced before we left so I didn't know why all the belts were now making music. I found a service station, hoping this would help me out. Well, it turned out they pulled the parts at two minutes to six.

The guy looks at me and he says, "They tightened the alternator fan belt so tight, it pulled the bearings outta line and wore down all the bearings on one side."

They would have to replace the alternator. The mechanic calls in just before they close, two minutes to go, and gets the alternator, puts it on, tightens it up to the right degree. And here we go! I paid all that money to have all this done at the original dealer and they tightened the fan belt improperly and I ended up having to get a new alternator.

And now I've got a thousand miles yet to go, and I'm driving here, most of it by night, on winding roads. And I remember feeling like that road got to looking to me like a big, long snake that just went off into the distance. You know, it was infinitely long. And I'm driving, trying to get there on time.

The last thousand miles, I was feeling frustrated

19

because we had already driven 1100 extra miles out of our way to avoid these icy conditions. We ended up getting hit by all the harsh ice, snow, and cold anyway. I felt like somehow something was keeping us from getting there. It was discouraging.

I finally get to Seattle, on time, so I can report for work when I said I was going to, on the eighth of February. At the downtown human resource center for Boeing, this old woman, probably in her sixties, takes me in.

And I walk up to the gal, and I say, "Here I am, I'm Allen Gliniewicz, I'm here and on the date that I was supposed to be."

And she says, "Oh, yeah. Oh, it's too bad that you didn't come here on Monday."

This was on a Wednesday. I just about flipped my cork. I was so mad.

I say, "You know, I traveled fifteen hundred miles in the last three days to be here on a date that I said I was going to be here, and I am here. I made it! We risked our lives in inclement weather, and you can't tell me it is too much trouble to move things, you know, from one column on the spreadsheet to another. You can't let me start the orientation today?"

I can't say that this made any difference at all just then…

So, I didn't go any further than that on that day. And that was my introduction to Boeing! [*Laughs.*]

I finally got to report to the engineering group that I was to work for at Boeing. And it turns out that the group was working on the Minuteman missile. Our group was working on airborne instrumentation, design, precise measurement, and troubleshooting of this equipment.

I was extremely fortunate to get a job with these people. I was one of three people, new guys that they hired, and the group we were to join were all probably the highest-qualified engineers in that Boeing division. I don't remember what the name of their division was, probably aerospace, something like that.

Most of the guys in my group had PhDs. And, certainly, the ones that didn't have PhDs had the equivalent of the experience in aerospace engineering. These guys were probably the highest-quality engineers available. I was very lucky to be a young and inexperienced engineer, now with a job in that group.

In addition to working with such accomplished engineers, our group had a lab of technicians under us that would do the work on the airborne instruments and prototypes that we tested.

These were the highest grade of technicians that there were at Boeing. And, besides that, we had a machine shop with A or B type machinists. A and B type machinists are ones that can work independently. The most skilled of the machinists were type A. In this way, the shop could make anything we wanted. We could just draw a diagram and give it to these people. They took that diagram and could fabricate whatever was needed or put together electrical circuits, anything like that.

As an instrumentation engineer, I was given the job of measuring dynamic pressures over experimental wing forms, and my responsibility was to decide how to calibrate instruments so that they would measure the pressures correctly. These measuring devices were known as pressure transducers and had to be fabricated especially in-house for us.

Additionally, I would have to troubleshoot data, if unexpected results happened in an experiment, simulation, or test flight. If we had flight data coming back from a test, for example a Minuteman missile test, and there was data that they couldn't explain, it became our job to explain it. And, before the explanation was ever made public, we had to prove with a laboratory test that our explanation was supported.

Boeing wouldn't publicize our results outside the group unless that was true – that our experiments were supported by our lab data. So, we were the engineers who were also responsible for designing tests to prove that our initial conclusions were right. There were several people in the group who had patents to their credit, including the manager. So, they were a top-quality group of engineers and it felt amazing to be part of this group with so many resources and such interesting and important work to do.

In addition to my regular tasks, I was supposed to build a simulator that would replicate the pressure environment between the first and second stages of the Minuteman missile. When the flying missiles had about a hundred thousand feet of altitude, the first-stage engine would extend, and the firing of the second-stage engine would happen. When it ignited, the space between the first and second-stage engines would begin to separate, and the side panels at the point of separation between the two stages would blow out and fall away. So, it'd have a partially contained explosion to accomplish this separation, while the second-stage engine fired.

In the test flight of the Minuteman, the pressure gauges were very important in our testing of all the phases of operation of the missile. The gauges ranged from very high to very low readings – I mean, they were built to read the pressures of the near vacuum of space which, of course, are quite low. There was always a question of how we could trust the data from those gauges after they'd been exposed to as high as 300 pounds of pressure per square inch.

So, you know, were these gauges going to give us any usable data? So, I was supposed to build a simulation for these pressure gauges for them and then we would check at the lab if they could do all the necessary tasks and read wide-ranging pressure values.

After a while, I guess they ran out of funding for pressure transducer experiments, and I got shifted within that group to the high-heat rate section. This newly assigned group was the top, the highest priority, and the dominant contractor working with Boeing in avionics. Avionics are all manner of electronic systems used on aircraft, including navigation, communications, etc. We were to work with the avionics on board the Minuteman II, and this was not a small task we had been given.

So, we would only get problems assigned to our lab when somebody was wanting to make a measurement or some type of experiment on a Minuteman missile and they couldn't solve the problem – for example, something unexplainable happened during a test, there was smoke released, or something burned. When Boeing was faced with these unsolvable problems and there was no one else to handle them, they got bumped up to us and we had to work on them. So, we only got the tough ones, problems that no one else could figure out. [*Laughs.*]

Whether it was an issue with heat, pressure, velocity – it could have been anything – they needed to have it explained. It then became our job to find the root cause of the issue, so that production could move forward. We had to either design an experiment to explain the problem, or modify some equipment to do the job, or invent something that would help explain the problem, and we did invent things.

One thing we invented is a device to measure extremely high heat. Because the Minuteman missile was launched from inside a concrete silo with a concrete cover, it had to withstand the heat of the rocket blast, which could be as high as the temperature of the flame of the rocket itself – the plume of the rocket engine. So, we had to have a good, high-temperature measuring device and a test apparatus to test it. We had such a device, and there was a lot of difficulty and controversy in building it. This controversy, I missed it. I was not part of the group when the device was developed, so I didn't know exactly what the issue was, but it had caused some problems among us. My group had developed a special protocol for working in the high-heat environment and a device that was better than anything else on the West Coast for the measurement of such temperatures in the launch silo of the Minuteman.

I was transferred to the job of keeping the extreme heat measuring device calibrated. We used optical, brightness, and temperature measurement devices for this purpose. Additionally, we had this device in constant circulation with the bureau standards being certified by them repeatedly, so that our readings were as accurate as possible. I learned how to operate and keep those things in calibration. I would perform certain heat-oriented tests that they might require to be done and see that the devices were accurate.

So, that was another thing I had to do. It's amazing, the high-heat measuring device. We built the thing, essentially, out of parts that were surplus – these were just lying around getting ready to get thrown away. With the help of an accomplished superior mechanical engineer, Heinz Riker, and an electrical engineer, Don Summer, I got to help refine the build of this device.

And it did work. As a matter of fact, a chief engineer at an instrument company paid me a visit and was asking me how I built it, because apparently his engineering staff couldn't do it. Our device could measure the heat at the separation point between the two stages of the Minuteman and measure the heat inside the concrete launch silo.

This sparked a response from me…

David: *Well, you had beginner's luck, you know*

Allen: [*Laughs*] If you don't think it's impossible, then you can do whatever you imagine. If nobody's told you it's impossible, then you just go ahead and do it.

25

They forgot to tell me that. [*Laughs*]

David

Right. I do that at work too – somebody tells me to do something, and I think about how to do it. I don't ask people, 'Oh, is this possible?' or whatever, I just go ahead and do it because I was told to do so.

I am extremely grateful to my dad for this quality. The way we dive into something just because we think we can do it, even if we don't know how we are going to. We just dive in with optimism and we don't give up until we accomplish whatever "impossible" task we have been given.

Computers without screen monitors, these are what was being used to do all the work and simulations at the time. It's incredible to me how everything was done without seeing anything on a screen.

Other work my dad did for Boeing was measuring pressures on experimental wing designs and the development of the SST. The SST was a supersonic transport plane. The SST was Boeing's response to the now-decommissioned Concord, which could fly from New York's JFK to London in two hours and fifty-two minutes.

Through all the development and work Boeing and my dad did on the SST, they found that the Concord was impractical, meaning the craft used too much fuel and was too expensive to be financially feasible. England and France's impetus to build the Concord was probably brought about by the space race and the desire to dominate the skies. This was further evidenced by the Russians developing their own supersonic transport, the Tupolev 144.

To make the Concord incredibly fast, the manufacturers were pushing the boundaries of flight and physics in the way spacecraft do, and we all know the ways in which spacecraft fail, as ultimately the Concord did.

Boeing, in the development of the SST, could not, of course, merely match the performance of the Concord, they had to beat it. This meant engines with insane amounts of thrust, which also meant that the engines were so heavy they would make the nose of the SST point up in the air. The heat demands on the SST as it traveled past the sound barrier were so high that body materials would have been too expensive. It would have needed to be made of titanium because the heat generated by such fast flight would melt traditional aluminum. Titanium is a material that is also more difficult to machine than aluminum.

Finally, if the SST were to be flying over the continental United States, they would be creating sonic booms regularly, which Americans did not favor. It would be like having the Blue Angels or Thunderbirds flying near our cities and neighborhoods, but much more often. Sonic booms can be loud enough to crack glass in structures on the ground.

For these many compelling reasons, SST development was abandoned by Boeing, and all the other supersonic transports as well. The Concord was living on borrowed time. History showed this later in the failure and crash in 2000 which killed 109 people, resulting in the retirement of the fleet in 2003.

Continuing now with my dad's words, he describes his personal and family life.

Allen

While in Seattle, the first three children were born. Leslie, she was the firstborn. And then Judy was born a year later. And David was born after another five years in 1967. All of you were born in Seattle. All of you were also quite different from one another – you were like islands unto yourselves.

Joan was in labor for nineteen hours delivering Leslie. Judy came into the world forty-five minutes after we stepped in the door of the maternity ward. Well, I don't remember the numbers on you, David, how long it was that your mom was in labor with you. It probably was not nineteen hours. That likely would have stuck with us if it had been.

David: *Maybe this is why I have never been interested in time.*

I don't know if you knew or not. You probably weren't watching the clock while you were being born. [*Laughs*]

But, anyway, two more incidents to report from the family side of things. One was on a weekend trip up to Olympic National Park. We eventually went up to the highest point – Hurricane Ridge, which rises about 6,600 feet above sea level. We were up there looking at the panoramic view which, of course, from that height it's easy to see.

As we are engrossed in the view, I happen to notice four-year-old Leslie is running around, down this long, sloping green. I became extremely anxious and upset because there was, farther down that way, eventually a 2000-foot drop. There was no sign to warn of the danger and no rails to prevent a fall from that harrowing drop. So, I started running after Leslie to catch her. In hindsight, I could have tried reverse psychology and turned around, walking the other way, but that would have been a gamble, if Leslie would have even seen this in time to get her to change her direction and would have started her running back the other way toward me.

I could feel my body was starting to surge with adrenaline just from running urgently down the hill. With this surge, it was probably more dangerous for me than it was for her at this point, just because I was then starting to panic.

I did catch up with her, got her, and dragged her back. Oh, she was crying due to the misunderstanding of the situation. To her, it was just a game of chase. I can't help but feel bad because I caused my child pain, though it was to save her from danger. It hurts too, though, because, of course, Leslie couldn't understand at that moment what was happening.

There was another trip that we made – to the Hoh Rainforest. It's the only rainforest in the continental United States – except maybe in Florida, who knows. This forest is near the Hoh Indian Reservation north of Aberdeen, Washington. We went there and we started out on a trip when it was raining, what a surprise [*winks*] – the fine Washington weather. So, we packed a lunch, and we sat down and gave everybody a sandwich. It was such a special place, with a lush and tranquil feeling. I felt grounded as we sat, eating our packed lunch in the rainforest, so near Indian land, I could feel the positive energy there.

The trees are so tightly packed together that when one dies and rots away, it can't even fall, it just leans against another tree, because there's no space for it to fall. In the rainforest, the moss hangs from the trees like big, green, heavy drapes, and the moss is over three feet deep on the ground. And when you step, it covers right over your feet as you walk. It was beautifully green.

I felt so at one with nature in this idyllic, primordial setting. I felt utterly whole and recharged – little did I know, nature was soon going to give me another type of feeling entirely.

Waaaalck waaaalck!

It was almost a crowish squawk, an aggressive sound that shattered my tranquil bubble.

My feeling of the soft buzz of nature had suddenly evaporated. I sat there, stunned, with my sandwich in my hand, as the bird berated me. I recoiled, feeling a bit like I was kicked out of paradise, and my communing with nature had taken an aggressive, predatory turn.

Maybe the Indian spirits were protecting their grounds, and this bird was the harbinger of some payback.

I guess the Canada jaybird was mad 'cause he or she wasn't getting any food. Apparently, the jay liked the pickle I gave him. I thought that was funny – the jay was mad because we had dared be in his space and not even offered any food.

David: [*Visualizing my dad and the angry bird scolding him*] *Jays are kind of obnoxious. We have some down in*

ALLEN and DAVID GLINIEWICZ

California too.

    Yeah, they're very noisy.

Houston

Allen

T his is now our journey to Houston. It seems like whenever we were making a transition, it was difficult every time [*laughs*] and this trip to Houston was no exception! The trip… it started out with me realizing that we were making a huge and sudden transition to go to NASA. And at that point, I had no idea what NASA was. And you were about six months old, David. You were born in March, and this was about September 1967 when we were moving.

I've just purchased a new car. I think that was one of the first new cars I ever had. It was a Dodge Cornet 440, and I didn't notice that it didn't have any air conditioning in it. And, you know, I was not about to take the family of five of us in a two-door hardtop on a 2,500-mile trip across the great American desert without having air conditioning.

Who sells a car without air? But things like A/C weren't standard in cars then.

I went up to the northern part of Seattle, where they

could do the installation.

And, lo and behold, they told me, "Oh, we're sorry, we don't have a kit that would work for your car, maybe because it's so new."

I let them know I needed it done urgently. So, they again checked the parts list, and the only difference in the kit they had was one fan belt that they had to install, and they finally did say okay.

If you've ever traveled through that area, it's beautiful, as long as you're within about fifty or sixty miles of the coast. After that, you're in the great American desert. There's not much growing anywhere there.

After crossing Washington State, we were quickly into that void in the eastern part of Oregon where it's just flat, desolate. I mean, it looks like a desert. And we traveled through that wasteland into Utah.

We saw this great big ship rock that was one of the few big landmarks there – a piece of rock the size of a whole ship. Something did start to happen at this point which we had to handle – the sound of crying.

David, you were generally a well-behaved baby, but you suddenly started crying. And you kept on crying and were bothered with something, and we didn't know what it was. We stopped at a friendly drug store when we were going through Provo, Utah, and asked the druggist, "Hey, is there something you can get that will help my kid?"

And they said, "Oh, yeah, there's some iron in the water that doesn't agree with kids and makes them cranky."

David: I happen to know now that iron can be constipating. That's why when you eat lots of steak you should also have a salad, or you will be in trouble. It's the iron in the steak wreaking havoc on your carnivorous bowels.

And he had something, some medicine, and he gave it to us. And thank God, you went right through the rest of the trip without any problem after that. You were just sleeping, then, for a long while. It was very helpful through the rest of Utah. We then traveled through what they call the Four Corners area, where four states come together in a little square which is marked on the ground on a monument. Colorado, Kansas, Arizona, and New Mexico, I believe.

We finally, after the fifth day, crossed the boundary into Del Rio, Texas, the absolute farthest-west part of Texas. We sort of limped on into Del Rio. We rested for a while there before we went on. We still had 700 miles to go to get to Houston. Texas is *that* big.

We finally made it to the Johnson Spacecraft Center. Those buildings are on a piece of land owned by Rice University. The space center had a special arrangement with the government so that Rice would let it at a very low rate, and the government could use that land for as long as they wanted, but with the stipulation that whatever buildings that they had and put up, they were going to leave for Rice.

David: I remembered the campus from my childhood visits there, and a later one we made together, that's why it doesn't look very impressive. It just kind of looks like office buildings, or it also does look like a college campus.

Allen: *Right. And I'm sure that that's why it was made that way, to go back to the institute eventually.*

I ought to digress and tell you why this whole situation existed, of how I came to be employed at NASA in the first place.

This story begins with a tragic accident with the Apollo One mission at NASA. Three astronauts were in a test chamber that was itself not flammable. The walls of the test chamber couldn't be burned, but they put enough equipment into it that when they were in a pure-oxygen environment, a fire ended up starting in the chamber due to the high level of oxygen burning up some of this equipment. NASA didn't plan a fast exit for the astronauts to escape the test chamber.

They couldn't get the doors open fast enough.

When the equipment inside the chamber started burning – things such as plastic – it created incomplete combustion products, which are compounds just hungry for oxygen. So, if you breathe any of this stuff, it gets into your bloodstream and then just combines with the oxygen on the surface of red blood cells.

Your blood cells are then incapable of carrying any further oxygen to the body. The only thing that can save your life at that point is a blood transfusion, and a fast one!

Unfortunately, the three astronauts all died, and of course, it was a real tragedy to the space program. In Washington, DC, NASA was told that obviously this was a danger, and that they didn't have adequate safeguards in place to prevent the accident. NASA was also told that they weren't doing good enough analyses of the high-risk situations, creating an unsafe environment for the astronauts. NASA then decided to get more engineering help to provide more safety for the operation, and that's when they gave a contract to Boeing, because NASA was not involved in the safety aspects after this point.

This reorganization in risk management was probably done for reasons of ethics and oversight. NASA had been trusted previously, though after such a failure their autonomy was reined in somewhat. NASA – under orders from Washington, DC – had requested that engineers be sent down to help them with their safety issues. I was one of those engineers, and that was called the TIE program, Technical Integration and Evaluation.

Well, the problem was that while we had had a good, easy relationship with the NASA engineers, when we finally got in there, the management felt that if they accepted the help we were wanting to provide, they were also accepting the responsibility for the deaths of those three astronauts. As a result of this misunderstanding, initially, the management – they were very reticent about working with us.

The staff at NASA did take our help, though one could sense this ease of cooperation was also accompanied by a feeling that perhaps – that they were forced to comply. This climate after the accident of Apollo One may have led to final repercussions that made life miserable for many people during this time.

I'm getting ahead of myself a bit. We didn't even have a place to stay when we came there. Due to the slapdash nature of how the Boeing engineers in the TIE program were sent to Houston, we didn't have a place set up for us to stay with our families. Boeing did give me a stipend for housing. They would pay for a month's stay at the Holiday Inn for the whole family. I and the rest of the family stayed there while we looked for a house during that time. The kids were going to school, so I had to take them to and from school, and that simple errand became a real task for a while. I guess I was showing signs of stress due to the emergent need for our help at Johnson.

I had to go to work, then come back, take them to school, and back to work again, you know. The TIE group were doing double shifts at the space center due to the urgent need for our group to handle the crisis and restore the safety of the space program. It was so exhausting to be in that role, thrown into an embarrassing crisis for NASA with fatalities, and being there to mop up and make sure it couldn't happen again.

All the while, I needed to be there for my family, as well. It was too much, the stress, but I wasn't aware how it was affecting me, I just kept doing my work the best I could.

David

Let me add that from the age of around two, or as early as I can remember, I was plagued by nightmarish images. These would continue nearly my whole time living in Houston. I escaped my crib at a very young age in flight of these phantasms. When I would wake, I would drowsily look at the shadow-filled wall of my room, only to see that the dream images had crossed over into my wakefulness. One of the images I still remember is that of a roaring lion. I only now know that it was a lion, since I was far too young to have known what that was.

One possible rationale for these continuing disturbances could be that I was channeling Allen's grief in dealing with the repercussions of the Apollo 1 tragedy.

I do tend to absorb the feelings of those around me, and I was especially close to my dad at that time.

One example of how I felt about my dad back then is that I would be upset if I missed him having breakfast before he went to work. Another reason I wanted to see my dad in the morning was that it gave me reprieve from my hellish nightmares.

Allen, however, being ambitious, would sometimes leave very early. He was always an early bird, being up many mornings at five a.m.

The other – and perhaps more frightening – interpretation of these nightmares and hallucinations is that the spirits of the Apollo 1 crew – who had passed away in flames – were sharing their torment and shock to have been wrenched from their bodies, and their anger at NASA for having set them ablaze in the one place they should have been safe, on the ground.

And now back to Allen's arrival in the dishevelment of NASA…

Allen

The Boeing personnel that I had come with, when we first came to Houston, we didn't have an office, either. We went to an off-site building on Saturn Lane. They hadn't decided where we were officially going to be located.

Which NASA group we were going to assist or how our group would integrate with the NASA program was not established. There was no coordination between the TIE program and NASA there at all. It was haphazard, to say the least. They finally put us with the flight mechanics division in Building 16, which happened to be the group of people who designed the launch-escape system.

This was a small rocket that sat on top of the command module, so that if anything went wrong during the first, early parts of the mission, explosive bolts would blow loose that would separate the command module from the rocket. The launch-escape rocket would also fire at this point, bringing the cargo of astronauts to safety should any hazards be present during the launch. It would remove the entire command module, which had separated from the rocket with the explosive bolts. The command module then would flip over, parachutes would come out, then it would hopefully land in water, safely away from the hazard.

Our system was built to land in water because the shock of hitting the ground could be so great, somebody could break their arm with the force of that kind of landing.

This is not at all what the space programs of other countries were doing. It was a lot more random where a craft might land, and they would let their craft land anywhere – farms, or woods!

Also, my work with all the Apollo missions was to ensure safe docking procedures for our own craft and those of other countries who were also developing spacecraft at the time. If we had a docking with a spacecraft from a foreign country, it was our hardware and the protocols we designed to make the docking possible, though NASA was nice enough not to mention this at the time, to the world, that we had designed the docking mechanisms, procedures, and protocols. We let other countries take credit for a joint mission.

One other thing about some foreign spacecraft of the period, if you will notice – some of the older craft were mostly spherically shaped. This is due to the fact that a sphere is a stable shape when dealing with pressure and stress, etc. It requires a lot of math calculations, testing, and simulating to make shapes that are different than a sphere and that have the needed strength. So, if you want a fast way to make a stable spacecraft – or a submarine, for that matter – then make a sphere.

Getting back to our discussion of improving safety at NASA. Our efforts and protocols became the standard for reducing risks. We ended up using this type of system throughout the rest of the missions, for safety's sake.

When we were housed in Building 16, and we also

had access to their computers, we were now fully incorporated into the culture of NASA. I would run simulations of a thousand cases of each scenario and each Apollo mission. The experiments were all different from one flight to the next because this Saturn rocket, which was thirty stories high, had a different weight distribution within each different rocket, for each mission. This was because every mission had different science experiments to be performed and would then, of course, have different equipment. NASA would plan how a given mission was going to fly. It would fly a little differently each time. And, of course, since the safety tests and the mission would involve parachutes, this also meant that the wind profile, with the changing weather, would vary from day to day. All these variables and the new ideas of all the most significant hazards which NASA came up with would also be part of the simulations. Where the "chutes" would take you would be different with a different wind profile.

I would run a thousand statistical studies and see that three-sigma statistical probability which would mean 99.9% of the cases for a flight that we were simulating would go the way we wanted it and would keep the astronauts safe. For the cases we would run, it would be assumed there was some sort of malfunction that we would then have to address.

Scenarios for us to test might be that the rocket would bump into the tower, or maybe some piece of equipment would turn during launch, or NASA would choose something to explode, and in tweaking the scenario they would then turn to us and ask, "Would they be all right?"

The new process of risk-management simulation was working well in preparing Apollo missions.

Apparently, about two weeks before every mission that I ran, NASA would suddenly pitch a suggestion for a failure, and I would run a simulation for the idea. It could be something like, "Oh, what happens if one of these doors should fall off?"

There were all kinds of cases. Once they would define a difficult situation, we had to prove that it couldn't happen.

Sometimes, during any launch, the rocket would pulse, and they were worried if the pulses got too great, could that cause the launch to get into some condition that would be dangerous?

[*Laughs.*] One of these scenarios was if the rocket, as it was launching – if it somehow got turned upside down and started flying inverted and then flipped sideways. Could it then fly right toward the blockhouse, which was where all the bigwigs of NASA were, and wipe them all out? [*Laughs.*] And they were happy when we proved that couldn't happen, either.

They had to wait two weeks before an actual launch to let us know what catastrophes were to be disproved. Then we had to run our simulations right away and prove that the failure couldn't happen for each mission scenario.

This process for each mission ran up until about 1969, when suddenly the priorities within NASA had shifted enough and there wasn't enough money for us to keep on doing this type of thing. The shift at NASA was beginning to lean in favor of unmanned missions, but this was only the almost imperceptible start of this shift. I received a more potent sign of what was about to happen within NASA, and it caused me to act.

I had an earth-shaking dream. I saw the NASA buildings and the sites at Johnson Spacecraft Center, and suddenly there was a terrific wind that blew huge boulders across and through the NASA buildings. And the boulders themselves were the size of the buildings. This was the destruction of NASA, and I was concerned about it. The dream was quite vivid, such that I could not stop thinking about it.

And I finally quit Boeing, which had my contract with NASA, and went to work for what I felt was the most stable company that I could.

This piqued my interest and a question in me...

David: *Do you think that dream that you had was kind of a warning? About the Apollo 13 crisis, or do you think it pertained to the loss of jobs?*

Apollo 13? No, I think it was about the cutting of funding.

This new company which I shifted over to was TRW Systems. This was also a company contracting with NASA. In 1969, I started doing scientific programming for them, which is mainly studying aborts and rendezvous trajectories around the moon, or various trajectories to the moon, or back and forth.

The docking and retrieval of equipment and satellites and other spacecraft's command modules, or from the surface of the moon, all these types of interfaces where problems could occur, these are the types of scenarios on which I worked and wrote software for onboard systems, or programs for troubleshooting spacecraft in flight.

One such program would soon get dusted off and put in the spotlight. During this time with TRW, this is when, suddenly, Apollo 13 occurred.

"Houston, we have a problem!"
- James Lovell, Apollo 13 astronaut

I got a call from NASA.

"We must run, Mater!"

Mater, in Latin, means mother. Let me explain what Mater is.

All the programming, at that time, was done on IBM punch-card computers, and I, along with another engineer, had written a program, which he let me name Mater. It was a program to test docking conditions prior to its use with Apollo 13. Mater wasn't even an official program, but something which allowed me to simulate the behavior of spacecraft – in this case, the Lunar Excursion Module, the LEM descent engine – landing on the moon, to see how the engine would cope with landing on the lunar surface.

The moon-landing simulations you see on old video games, from the 70s and 80s, this is the same type of software simulating the thrust of the LEM. We had a real accident onboard Apollo 13. We had never simulated this type of event before. NASA had felt, up to this point, that the possibility of a deep-space emergency like the one that happened was so remote that they didn't even consider the possibility as anything worth devoting resources to – they didn't even simulate it.

In defense of NASA, they certainly could not prepare for every type of failure.

And the actual thing that happened, which ended up causing the explosion, was that somehow the little electronic valve system that turned the oxygen generator on and off, that switch normally operated at just 28 volts. Well, somehow in the manufacture of that group of circuits, the circuit ended up becoming over voltage because there was an unintended connection with a higher-voltage circuit. This higher-voltage circuit had somehow temporarily connected to the 28-volt oxygen-generator circuit.

The result of this unintended, temporary connection was that it welded contacts together that were of very different voltages. The circuit which had been 28 volts was changed and was operating beyond its safe voltage. This situation was not caught, and that thing was put into the rocket, unfortunately.

The bad, now over-voltage, connection was always generating more and more oxygen, and there wasn't a place for it to go. So, the pressure was building up inside the vessel, all during the trip. And finally, when Apollo 13 gets a hundred miles from the moon, the over-manufacturing of oxygen finally exceeds the strength of the vessel that was supposed to contain it. The oxygen compartment explodes into a thousand different shards, many different fragments all go in various directions, and they damage the control cables so badly that, of course, they cannot be repaired.

The only rocket engines that could normally maneuver the spacecraft around and bring it back were destroyed. So, they had a real problem. And if you see the pictures of that thing, it blew so hard that it blew a panel right out of the side of the vehicle. It was like a jagged new door opened into space. The explosion cut everything… all the control cables. The saving grace was that the LEM, with its descent engine, was in a different compartment, and it was now the only rocket engine on board that could be steered.

If the LEM's engine could be used, steering would be with great difficulty, as the damaged new configuration of the spacecraft was not intended to fly in this new, improvised way. The LEM was small, with an engine a lot smaller than the command-module engine. It was only built to land the LEM on the moon. NASA control didn't know if the LEM engine could deliver enough thrust, even if they could somehow get the crippled spacecraft in the right position, to bend the trajectory and slingshot around the back of the moon.

The question on everyone's minds in control became, *could the LEM engine also give the needed thrust and come back all the way to Earth?*

So, that was what my job now was, to take Mater, the stripped-down and anonymous program, and see if the LEM's little rocket engine could deliver enough thrust to take the entire configuration of vehicles around the back of the moon, using the gravity of the moon to slingshot back.

Could this improvised alternative rocket engine

turn the trajectory enough to get the astronauts back to Earth? The answer to this critical question is what the Mater program was able to provide, and it was on a deck of cards sitting there for probably about six months.

The computers used for simulation and calculation at NASA all had programs with data that were on punch cards. Because there were no magnetic media at the time, such as tape or disk drives, all the data was stored on punch cards. The punch cards were then put, in order, into a card reader and it was then sent, now in the form of a program, to the computer, which was most likely an IBM 704.

This anonymous program answered the question of whether a rescue of the Apollo 13 crew was possible at all. It was sitting on the card reader equipment because it was not an official program, and it was not documented anywhere. I just happened to know where it was and ran it. The problem with punch-card input programs is that they can have a hanging chad, like the one that caused the voting problems years ago, which cost Al Gore an election. There were card-sorting machines which could help locate card errors before inputting into the computer, though the deck was run without going through the sorter. The deck ran fine the first time without any errors, and we had a result – the LEM could make it back!

This was the beginning of the Apollo 13 rescue effort and perhaps NASA's finest moment.

There were many other challenges along the journey of Apollo 13 back home, such as surviving without heat, filtering toxic carbon dioxide out of the craft's air supply, and booting the reentry capsule's computer and jettisoning the damaged command module.

Apollo 13, the film, was a great portrayal of all these challenges and how they were overcome one by one.

David

After the rescue was complete and Apollo 13 was home, my dad and all the NASA staff responsible for the rescue were given a mission coin which was about the size of a quarter. It had the NASA insignia on one side and the Apollo 13 craft and trajectory on the other.

I confess I lost this coin, or maybe even gave it away, not knowing its significance, when I was in third or fourth grade.

You see, my dad did not talk about his accomplishments or the events at NASA at all. Of course, all activities at NASA were covered by a security clearance and Al was legally bound to not talk about all the adventures, struggles, and victories that happened in his career there.

Much later, when my dad was looking for the mission coin, I told him what had happened and that I had lost it. I wanted to make it up to him and bought two coins at online auctions. These were both quite expensive and were showy commemorations, though they were not exactly like the mission coin. The mission coin was more modest looking, an insider, sentimental gesture by NASA that cemented a bond of excellence against incredible odds.

The accomplishment of the rescue was an example of climbing the glass mountain, using tools – such as Mater –

which were forged in the technological realm of NASA to achieve the Apollo 13 rescue. And the application of Mater was like the mythic eagle or mountain lion who lent their specialized gifts to us mere mortals.

The use of the unique gifts of Mater, something no other tool could have given us at that moment, brought us to the summit, another seemingly impossible goal reached.

We had an event which underscored Allen's contributions at NASA. It was 2018. Al, his girlfriend, Gloria, and my wife, Ellen, and I visited Johnson Space Center. My dad hadn't been at the center since his work there with Apollo 13. He was now eighty-four.

The center was, in addition to being a working space command center, also now a huge tourist draw. We took the tour, and it ended in the display hangar building of the immense thirty-story Saturn rocket, which was exhibited on its side.

I had lost track of Ellen, and I went to find her in the crowd at the exhibit. I had left Allen alone on a bench as I went to find Ellen. When I came back, Al had an audience of maybe six to eight people around him, who were listening intently to how he had worked in the grounds of the space center, and what he had done with the Saturn rockets and the Apollo program.

So often when we level up, we leave our safe environment and go somewhere we can be challenged and where we can grow. Houston was no longer a place in which growth was going to happen easily. It was becoming economically stagnant. A visit to our old neighborhood, a mile or so from Johnson, would illustrate the economic collapse which was closing in on Houston.

We used to live in Seabrook, an oh-so-short drive from the space center and right on the water of the Gulf of Mexico. Seabrook is where all the staff of the space center lived. You could almost walk to work from the neighborhood.

That area of Seabrook looked as if there had been a time warp. It was still in the same condition that it had been when I was five years old, except for some aging and unkind wear.

There was a strip mall a block from our house on El Mar Lane. It was a modest-sized mall with maybe four stores, including a drug store – which had a diner. As kids, we were so amazed that we could walk in and get free ice water. As hot as it was there in Houston, I felt like I had won the lottery when the cool, frosted glass was set in front of me.

The sidewalk of the strip mall was about four steps up from the gravel driveway and parking area and stretched the length of the store fronts. There was another separate building to the left of the strip mall which, when I lived there, was a five-and-ten where you could find all sorts of toys.

After first going to the drug store for a cool glass of water, me and my friend Danny would walk down the length of the sidewalk toward the five-and-ten. Where the storefront ended, the sidewalk did also, and we would then jump down from where the sidewalk dropped off to the pavement, three feet down, and go over to the five-and-ten.

You would think, in the time between 1973 and 2018, the configuration of this strip mall and the buildings there would have had some growth and change. Growth is something we should certainly expect from a place that was the leader in space exploration, like all busy industrial and technological areas.

When I saw that strip mall looking nearly identical to the

way it had been when I was five, 51 years ago, I understood that my dad's dream was right, and that the economy of the area was stagnant for more than fifty years.

Allen

My family's transition to Pennsylvania began with the end of the golden age of space flight in Houston in the 70s.

TRW ended up losing its contract with NASA. They lost it to McDonald Douglas, who had drastically underbid them. The landscape of opportunity for aerospace jobs was drying up in Houston.

McDonald Douglas, just to get the contract with NASA, likely hired the cheapest engineers that were available, the newer college graduates.

Meanwhile, at TRW, our people argued with the management and said, you know that they're going to have to raise the cost of this contract to make money, there is no way we can do it at this price! TRW was up against a wall because of the pressure from McDonald Douglas with their extreme low-ball bid. TRW didn't want to back down, but they were in a corner...So, unfortunately, they forced us out.

Clarence Pittman, who was the manager of Houston operations for TRW, got up before all the TRW employees and said, "Does anybody have any ideas about how we are going to take care of our people in this crisis?"

I came up with an idea and I said to the group,

"Well, I just saw an ad that said TRW bought a new subsidiary company within the Houston area called TRA Controls. Maybe our engineers could find work with them." This company built small computers to control things like power plants, water filtering systems, and chemical and manufacturing plants. Another business TRA Controls worked in, and this was a huge business in Texas, was servicing the petrochemical industry.

We were in Houston, after all, where oil is the name of the game!

I went on to say that we could write more powerful programs than the average engineers. We could use these more-powerful computers from TRA Controls to build control systems for water distribution or water treatment systems. Of course, all the small towns had to treat their water, because there were a lot of minerals in the water in Texas.

I figured our engineers could do all that work with these control systems on these new and fast computers that TRW had just acquired from TRA to build control systems for not only water, electrical power, and natural gas, but even for trains and other public transport. That was the answer we were all looking for to save us!

And so, TRW started a whole new area of business that day, but the new opportunities with this plan couldn't include all the employees whose jobs hung in the balance, though a great many did benefit from this new plan, including me.

While working in this new role, I wrote an alarm processor for the WMATA Rapid Transit System in

Washington. I was using the TRA processing computer system to write a program that handled controls and alarms for emergencies on the trains, and to handle these emergencies correctly and quickly enough to avoid death or injury.

David: A side note, and perhaps a recurring theme in Allen's life, is that "Mata" also means mother. I think God has a great sense of humor!

With the control system of the train, if something happened, the alarm processor had to be able to put together a message to warn the operator that there was something wrong, and what to do about it to avoid passenger injury.

I looked at the messages that needed to be sent to the driver of the train. These, of course, varied to each emergent situation that might happen. The appropriate message had to reach the driver within seconds so that the driver could then take corrective action. The error messages were stored on magnetic tape like a cassette music player.

It seemed like an impossible situation, due to the number of different messages to handle the various types of accidents and hazards. I couldn't suddenly put all these messages in at the time an accident was happening and have it read by the computer. With this method of input from the tape, it could take five minutes to read the data from the cassette, and of course this would have been far too late to avoid any trouble.

So, I figured out that if I looked at all the messages

that there were, maybe I could break them into six parts. Let's say we are breaking the phrases of the warning messages into six words or short phrases, so they can be assembled from memory very quickly and sent to the operator.

I made tables inside the memory of the computer for each one of those six parts of the error messages, and all the possible parts of the warning message were contained in this table. I labeled each cell of the table with the individual error messages, giving each one a unique number.

So, I invented that method to use in core memory. The table inside provides great speed for accessing the data in the cells. And all this to accomplish getting the error message to the operator in milliseconds rather than minutes, making the trains extremely safe.

The computer would get an error code based on a trigger caused by an event – for instance, a door staying open, or proximity to another train. Let's say this code is, for example, 543621.

The computer would then assemble the warning message from the text and phrases stored in the memory cells with the labels 543621 and send them to the operator.

For instance, warnings could be, "Close rear car door before moving the train!" or "Stop train due to switch issue," or "Train detected ahead! Reduce speed now!"

I think they modified the system I had made before it was put in use. They souped it up a little bit more.

Having a working system for the trains meant it was

the end of the contract for this job for the WMATA system. It was 1974. I would be going to work for GE in Pennsylvania after this contract.

A few things to note before closing the chapter on Houston. There were two more additions to the family prior to leaving – Melissa and Leah, two more daughters. Melissa was born in September of 1971. Leah was born two years later in May, and they were unexpected. We did have a comfortable life and routine in Seabrook. The family enjoyed a pool in the neighborhood, which was so needed in that infernal Houston summer heat.

Also in Seabrook there were hurricane scares! The neighborhood was once under warning from a hurricane coming in from the gulf, which was unusual because the gulf naturally shields the area from hurricanes. Under this warning, the residents boarded up their windows and were ready to leave town if the signal was given.

David

Leslie, Judy, and I remember this hurricane scare. The sky turned yellow as the hurricane approached landfall from the bay, and the wind blew about 75 miles per hour, which is weak for a hurricane. After maybe twenty minutes or so, the yellow color of the skies returned to the usual hazy blue and the winds died down again, like nothing at all had happened.

Leslie and Judy had a friend, Amelia, whose dad owned a local restaurant out by the bay, a few blocks from our place in

Seabrook. His restaurant shared his last name, spelled M-U-E-K-E and pronounced Micky.

The feeling at Mueke's was like a kid's first time at Disneyland.

Inside, it was a cozy place. The bar had figures and trains carved from Budweiser cans. On the wall was an electronic dart board where patrons would tap a button on the remote to "throw" darts. When the darts were launched this way, little illuminated projectiles would appear on the dartboard. It was amazingly cool tech for 1970.

Some nights, Mr. Mueke would fire coffee cans out of a cannon which stood guard outside the entrance to the bar. The Folgers can would arc out over the bay.

Amelia and her dad were colorful people, and anyone near them was drawn in by their laughter, and would be at ease, with a laugh of their own soon enough. Leslie, Judy, and Amelia were great friends, though somehow, we all lost touch after we left Houston.

The prosperity of Mueke's was a sign of the times – the NASA staff were all nearby, coming to blow off steam from the pressure cooker at work, and the cash and beer flowed easily there, until it didn't. Probably when things changed at NASA.

I often wonder what happened to Amelia and her dad. When visiting Seabrook much later, the restaurant was gone. It had been replaced by gulf-side housing. This newer house was perched high on stilts, like many of the buildings there. This was to avoid the floods which could sometimes happen. As I thought back on the place where the waterfront house now stood, I didn't think Mueke's restaurant had been up off the ground, which might have meant it got flooded at one point.

ALLEN and DAVID GLINIEWICZ

To fight the economic lull in the aerospace industry, Allen then scrambled to go where the higher-paying, more rewarding, and growing work was. There was a mass exodus from Houston, which was escalating. Al leaving was a means to provide for his family, which had now grown to seven.

My mom was also struggling with the pressure of caring for her many children.

It was necessary for our family to move to Pennsylvania.

Much later, in 2018, when I saw Seabrook unchanged by so many years, I understood that it had been the right choice, and that if we had stayed, we would not have had the opportunities we have, nor the quality of life we enjoy.

Pennsylvania

Allen

I started working for General Electric, which had a huge – you could say *palatial* – facility in King of Prussia, PA. This was June 1974, and I came up by myself because we couldn't sell the house in Houston. It wasn't a good market in Texas for selling at the time – people weren't moving around so much and selling their houses.

I had to just leave and come up to PA, cause GE... they did want me up here right away.

So, I did come. However, when I did, there was an extensive processing and intake procedure where we all were just held in an area for several months. GE did give us stuff to do during this time, though it was not related to the job. I mean, in only a very small way was it related.

The housing situation here was a lot tougher for me to get a place. There were established communities already, and very few new houses, or any open houses that you could buy in the area.

The neighborhoods were quite different. All the

streets were laid out like in colonial times. They were all close together.

It's not a small decision, to try to figure out where you want to live, you know...

So, there was no easy way to just pick a place to live and move there. As a matter of fact, I spent the first five months living in the basement room of a realtor's house in the area.

The owner had a friendly dog that was always looking in at the basement window, and he just wanted to come in, and wanted to so badly. Finally, one day he just broke through the window. [*Laughs.*] Oh, he came through, all right! So, that was a bit of an issue. I guess maybe when someone wasn't living there it was probably the dog's little place, and it was as if he was saying, "Hey, let me show you how I really enjoy lying on this bed the entire day."

I eventually found a rental place there, a house where we could all stay, and this is also when the house down in Houston finally sold.

Joanie could finally come up with the children to Pennsylvania, to a little town called Paoli, which was forty-five minutes west of Philadelphia on what was called the Main Line, named after the train route from the city.

Then we stayed in that rental house that was on Kent Lane. And you probably remember that place...

David: [*A chill ran through me*] I do. Yeah. I-I felt it was haunted! Honestly...

Allen: *You felt what?*

David

I felt it was haunted. I used to hear footsteps up and down the stairs at night...

I recounted the events in my mind... Hearing these percussive sounds and thinking one of my sisters had decided to get some rapid cardio in at two a.m., I ran out to look at who it was bounding up and down at a brisk pace, with a slight pause at the top and bottom of the stairs. Once I got out on the landing, near the stairway, the sound of urgent footfalls would stop.

The first time these events played out, I paused on the landing, incredulously, looking for the source of the sounds, seeing none, and waiting in dread for them to return. As I have heard from many supernatural accounts – and from my own, later experiences – when I heard the footfalls, I also felt the presence of what I thought was a person and was, of course, shocked not to find anyone.

Confused and alarmed during my pause on the landing, my sense of danger would give way to doubt that I'd ever heard anything. I would then go back into my room. After settling down in my bed and relaxing again, and just as the last traces of the bizarre events had left my mind and sleep was creeping back upon me, I would hear the bump-bump-bump of those footfalls again. This tedious and annoying haunting continued through many nights there. The phenomenon did seem to taper off eventually, maybe, or maybe I just stopped paying attention. I may have blocked the events out of my mind to carry on some semblance of normal life, and to avoid thinking about those footstep sounds in the night.

I was so glad to leave that place as soon as we did.

Allen: Remember the underground bomb shelter that was left over from the old war days? Did you kids ever go in and play down there…?

No, I was never able to go into that bomb shelter. It felt like going into a gravesite or something, with that plywood sheet covering the hole and just being blacker than the already dark, dingy shade of the basement. The farther down you went, the less you could see.

All Leslie, Judy, and I could manage was to lift the plywood and look down. None of us could muster the nerve to descend the rough-hewn steps – to the bowels of the earth, it seemed.

Aside from that horrible bomb shelter, we did have the train set down there, you know, that old antique Lionel train set, it was there, and, of course, I would wanna play with it…and I would, for a while… That is, until I realized I was alone in the basement. At that point, I would get overwhelmed by fear and anxiety, though still trying to play. I had a habit of holding my breath in situations like those.

I was also terrified of something otherworldly coming to get me! I just became really creeped out after playing for a little time in that basement. And I would just have to leave there, in a kind of blind and anxious bolt. I would run out of there as fast as I could.

I just had a rattlingly bad feeling down there. I don't know what it was, but it was palpable, we all felt it. I was six years old at the time.

A short time later, Leslie and Judy began to talk about and share their interest in ghosts. I was even caught up in that to a degree, or maybe more than I thought. I guess it was a

61

way to stave off the fear, by having a fascination with the spirit realm in one way or another, that felt more positive somehow.

Maybe this is the same reason we watch horror films. We watch scary movies from a safe place, usually with someone we love. In this way, we feel like we face our fears, to some degree. I know I would do anything not to hear those footfalls in the night or that prickling of goosebumps and the palpitations that came with them.

When I then went to the library at school, I would look at books of ghosts. And when we ordered books from the Scholastic book fair in our class, it wasn't sports or comedy I chose, but The Amityville Horror, a book where on the cover it has the tagline, "This book will scare the Hell out of you!"

Siblings often engage in ongoing jokes with one another. Leslie and Judy had become particularly skilled at this after our eerie experiences in the basement, as well as the mysterious footsteps that echoed through the stairs every night. These pranks had taken on a supernatural theme, as I would soon see.

I came into their room one day and they had a table lamp turned on. It sat on the dresser.

"There's something going on with the lamp! I think it's a ghost or something," said Judy.

"I think it's haunted," Leslie told me. She turned to the lamp. "Do you communicate at night only? Blink once for yes, and twice for no."

The light blinked once.

They both began asking questions to the lamp, and each time it would blink as an appropriate response to the question. This went on for several minutes and I was amazed, and somehow thrilled inexplicably. I think I even asked some questions, which the lamp answered, blinking spritely.

Then Leslie and Judy laughed, and I hadn't noticed Leslie's hand under a throw pillow. She took her hand from under the pillow and showed me the corded remote dimmer. This dimmer was how she was controlling the light. I had been punked again.

I was not upset about being pranked. I was more let down by the fact that the seemingly possessed blinking light was not a supernatural phenomenon. I guess I had felt the lighthearted questions that Leslie and Judy were asking the light meant that the spirit possessing the lamp was a friendly ghost, like Casper.

Allen

I didn't like the place on Kent Lane, either. I'm glad we were able to get out of there too. It took us a while to locate a house, and the place we ended up getting was one that belonged to a veteran, a GI I had befriended at an army and navy surplus store in downtown Paoli.

The house was on Russell Road in Paoli. It had become too big for the GI – he was disabled and used a wheelchair. As a fellow GI, he took pity on me, with my then-fruitless search for a house for me and my family, and he sold me his home. It was a four-bedroom house with a full basement and double garage. Also, the place had an unfinished attic, which we later made into another bedroom.

I remember going to visit that house for the first time. There was wallpaper in every room. I went up to the hot, dusty attic. There was a mummified bat, shriveled like a raisin, on the floor near the window. I kicked the brittle bat over to where the rough planks of the unfinished floor ended and into the space between the walls. It fell with a crackle like a dried leaf.

David

My dad's friend Mike and I helped steam and peel the wallpaper from every room. Even the closets had wallpaper holding fast to every surface. It took a few weeks, and it felt like forever. Allen: Yeah, it was a nice, big house, and eventually we remodeled it and made it livable. There were some issues, though. For instance, in many places there was no subflooring.

Remembering the house, how it readily transmitted sounds, I said... So, no wonder you could hear everything anyone was doing on the floor above you. If you were in one of the bedrooms, you knew what was going on above you, you could just hear that well.

Allen and I were glad to move on from the talk of the houses in Paoli, though there were some limitations that Al had to mention regarding his job. This was due to issues of security.

Allen

I will have to say that I can't discuss what I did at GE, unfortunately.

ALLEN and DAVID GLINIEWICZ

I did have the freedom working there that I could run at lunchtime around the rolling green hills of the campus for forty-five minutes. And they had a nice shower for employee use. And so, I got to run often and eventually worked my way up to five miles a day.

I know this maybe isn't as juicy a story as with my prior work in the space program.

One amazing thing about working with GE was the training you could get from them. I eventually started what was called the ABC Course. This was engineering training with actual college credit. I'd always had on-the-job training wherever I had worked before, but I never had gotten any degree credits for all the work that I did.

These courses were a great opportunity, and I decided I was all-in. I wanted to get credit toward a degree. And this course – not only was it the highest-level, most difficult, challenging thing in technical engineering, but it could end up giving me either a master's degree or a PhD, depending on how ambitious I was. So, I decided to try it. The course was three academic years.

And it was grueling, because each week we had a three-hour lecture Fridays, nine p.m. until midnight. We got a lecture and then we got a problem, and we had to solve it and have a full engineering report written to get into the next lecture.

By the third year, the C portion of the course, I was a full-time graduate student with a full load of amped-up, arduous courses.

And I was so tired when I was working with that

course load. I noticed that, even though I was sitting in the front row of the lecture hall, the blackboard just went out of focus on me. So, thinking I was reaching my limit, I backed off a bit and just tried for a master's degree.

I guess that's what happens when I'm already working sixty hours a week. So, it was twenty-four, twenty-five hours on top of that.

I did have a sense of accomplishment. Over the thirteen years that I worked at GE, I went from a grade-four rated engineer – this was with credit for four years of experience when I started – to a grade-thirteen ranked engineer by the time I left.

David

I had no idea what my dad was doing at GE. As a ten-year-old at the time, I thought he was working on refrigerators and microwaves, that's all I knew from seeing the name on our household appliances. Little did I know the company included aerospace and so many other highly technical divisions.

The GE campus where Allen worked was also built several floors underground, so most activities at the center were not public knowledge.

Al, of course, was bound by a security clearance to not disclose any information about his work.

It was also funny later. When my dad mentioned to ten-year-old me that he was maybe getting a PhD and going to be a doctor, you can imagine what kind of doctor I thought he was going to be. This further confused me because I couldn't fathom how my dad suddenly got into the medical field.

ALLEN and DAVID GLINIEWICZ

It was unfortunate too, as happens with talented people in technical careers, that they are in high demand and their time is limited. Allen was so busy that there was not an opportunity to discuss and straighten out the matter of whether he was now a medical doctor or not. I even mentioned this at one point, to one of my sisters. I think it was Leslie. "Dad's going to get his PhD and be a doctor!" Leslie just looked at me incredulously and probably thought I was crazy.

Allen would soon be needing a medical doctor's help, actually.

When my dad was in the army in West Germany, salt pills – the equivalent of Gatorade – were given to the troops to limit heat stroke. Drinks with added salt are what sports drinks are – "electrolyte ingredients" is just a fancy way to say salt has been added.

So, Al was in the habit of taking salt pills when he felt heat fatigue.

I happen to know too, since I had my own stressful medical career, that it is a stress response when you crave salt.

Allen's cravings were so serious that he even drilled the holes in the saltshaker to be larger to allow more of the tang and zest of salt to teem onto his food.

There was a downslope in the backyard of our house, which tended to become overgrown with blackberries, poison ivy, and other vines, trees, and shrubs.

One particularly hot day, my dad decided he wanted to dig a flat terrace into the side of the hill to make a usable area on the wild, overgrown slope. He took some preemptive salt pills and went out to dig in the hot sun.

I had been playing up the street with some friends when Leslie came up to us and said, "Dad collapsed in the backyard and said he's having a huge pain in his side. His face went white and he's not moving!"

He was taken to the hospital, and they found a kidney stone.

Allen: I finally realized that running was aggravating the kidney stones. I had extreme lower-back pain. I felt I could almost *count* the stones going through me. So, I knew that when I was doing certain things, like running, I was forming stones. I knew too I had clues as to what I needed to avoid – salt pills, for example.

David: At this point during our interview, I couldn't help but let my knowledge of kidney pathology kick in. This was from my fifteen-year career in radiology, and it spewed forth. I'm not a doctor, but I do know a lot about the body.

That's true! The kidneys aren't anchored to anything like other organs or bones, they are just suspended near your lower back. They're sort of floating in fat. If you're running, they're always in motion, and even if you aren't making stones, you make sort of… micro injuries to your kidneys just by running, with that up-and-down motion.

And, you can have blood from the little stones getting shaken up even on a microscopic level as you run. Riding a motorcycle can also do the same thing in shaking the kidneys.

Allen

After recovering, I took it a lot easier. It was uneventful, for a while, for me. You and your sisters were mostly in school or working during this time. Leslie was in art college, Judy was modelling, Melissa was in junior college. David, you had graduated from art school, and Leah was also in college. You were all in school at nearly the same time.

After GE, I worked for Pacer Systems. For them, I wrote a narrow-band acoustic processor software for anti-submarine-warfare use. I learned the C programming language over the weekend to be able to do that. [*Laughs.*]

David: *Tell me more about what you were doing with Pacer?*

Well, we were trying to detect the presence of Russian submarines. They would make a marine recording of the sounds coming from vehicle traffic going by down there. And they would highlight what the target sounds were that they wanted to pinpoint and for the software to report.

So, they'd give me a sample of what they were looking for, and I didn't even know what the sounds were at that point – it didn't matter all that much if I did.

I wrote it in a flexible way. They could just put in any recorded or livestream sound feed they wanted, and it would be stored in memory buffers – these are discrete areas of memory storage. The more sounds were put in, the more buffers would be created.

Sounds in buffers could then be searched and matched to whatever sounds were being targeted.

I was able to get the program to run fast enough. So, the users or crew on a boat who were looking for Russian subs, they never had to stop the recording from below the surface of the water. The inflow of sound from under the ocean would just keep running into the computer buffers continuously, and get processed on the fly as well, matching to the targeted sounds and flagging if a match was found.

It was able to run on an ordinary PC that could be put anywhere. Any sound could be fed through to the buffers as the equipment and vehicles they were looking for changed, and any new type of sound could be searched. It was not limited to submarines, of course. The sounds could be from something else, like marine life, or anything you could record.

There was also a war-gaming system, which was built to train naval commanders, teaching them how to allocate their forces and move them around. And it simulated the movement of a vessel and even quite sophisticated ships, like aircraft carriers.

The software would calculate the time it would take to move airplanes up and down the elevators of the aircraft carrier, while also simulating enemies firing torpedoes at it, calculating the probability of the ship becoming disabled as well. It was simulated to quite a high degree, as realistically as possible.

But the software was really second-rate. I mean, it was bad. There were a lot of problems with it. The software showed a visual representation of the activity on a monitor just like any video game. But the war game wasn't smart enough to know the difference between a vehicle moving on land or in the ocean, cruising through water.

On the day of the software presentation, I was in there trying to offer technical support, if anyone had questions during the testing. On the monitor of the war game, we had an image of Africa, and there was a ship sailing right through the Sahara – you know, not a good look!

A little kid, one of the managers' children, happened to walk up to see the monitor display. He asked incredulously, "What is it doing?" He pointed to a ship that had grown legs.

I was too embarrassed to explain how stupid the program was. [*Laughs.*]

So, I just got up and left at that point.

I was surprised by this because I knew my dad did only high-quality work.
David: *But it wasn't your doing. I mean, you didn't write that program.*

No, it was some other company. I didn't program it.

It was made by someone else, but fortunately, they had picked me to go to San Diego and to demonstrate this software for evaluation. This was for some of the tactical people in the navy who were honing their skill in facing enemies. These naval staff had their lives on the line, and they wanted to make sure they maintained their edge. They wanted to know, of course, if this software would do anything to help them in their goal to prepare for combat.

And the simulation software had such major, glaring issues. The SI staff, me, and the rest of my group, we didn't feel good about it.

Later, I happened to be sitting, and one of the chiefs, a tactician, came and asked me, "How do I do this?" It was a certain critical operation needed in battle.

I said, "I'm sorry, the program can't do that." [*Laughs.*]

And then he asked, "Well, how about doing this?" about another critical battle requirement.

"It can't do that, either," I replied.

My role there… I was part of the SI staff, the system integrators, who worked between the military and the vendors trying to sell the software.

Our group, including me, said, "No, we're not recommending that the navy buy this thing."

And he looked at me and I said, "That's right! We aren't backing this thing."

You see, somebody way on high was ordering evaluation of the gaming system and allowing the evaluation to be kept alive, even though the system was a piece of junk.

And, when I said that, the chief eventually told the commander of the ship, the tactical lead, and he was a guy with some backbone.

He said, "We are not putting this piece of crap on my ship."

The board that was evaluating the gaming simulation finally got back to somebody with some authority in the hierarchy of the naval command. I heard after I left that the naval administrator was demoted for his actions, for trying to push through that crap software.

David: [*With a feeling of amusement] Were you working for the software company, and saying not to buy the* *product? Is that what happened?*

Allen: *Well, there were two sides to it. Half the group was trying to manufacture this thing. And I was part of the SI staff.*

David: *Oh, okay. So, you were an independent contractor, you weren't on anybody's side?*

Allen: *Well, I was working for the war-gaming software company, actually.*

David: *That's hilarious. I love it. "You don't wanna buy our software, it sucks!"*

[Both laughed.]

Another place I worked, I don't think they are around anymore, was Rosenbluth Travel. I was working on their Y2K stuff for their reservation system.

I guess I was a little too good at that contract job. Their computer reservation system's new ease of use made many of the employees unnecessary.

Rosenbluth sold the company and laid off all the employees. With online booking, their days were numbered, anyway, so it's just as well it played out this way.

I did feel bad for all the people who were laid off, and since it was right after I worked with them, I felt a bit responsible for that, somehow.

David

Another transition was about to take place, and my dad found work down in Atlanta, Georgia.

Prior to leaving PA, however, there were some issues which needed to be handled. A health crisis was brewing for Allen. This issue would follow him down to Georgia.

Atlanta

Allen

I t was extremely difficult for me to decide to come down to work in Atlanta. It was the best money I'd ever been offered. It turned out to be a one-year consulting job with Delta Airlines.

Just prior to this point, I had partially undiagnosed prostate cancer. As far as the doctors were concerned, I had prostate cancer, but they were unable to get a positive biopsy to make it a clear and actionable diagnosis. And, without the formal diagnosis, the insurance wouldn't cover any kind of preparatory or invasive procedures. So, I was stuck with cancer and had no way to treat it!

I was in Paoli at the time, and I tried to interest the Fox Chase Cancer Center in taking my case. The doctors at the center told me I would have to wait a month before they would even look at me. And I was afraid that I had advanced prostate cancer, and that it was aggressive. And I was afraid I'd be dead soon... that I wouldn't make it a month. So, since nothing was happening with my treatment, I decided to take a chance and go down to Atlanta. I packed up everything and decided to drive down there.

I started early in the morning. It was February of 1999.

I drove down there in one hop, and it's a long drive. I pulled into my first view of Atlanta at a quarter of twelve at night.

I was absolutely dazzled. That city is beautiful. It's one of the most beautiful cities in the United States when it's lit up. And I felt buoyant and cheered on seeing that sparkling city. The night lighting down there was spectacular!

But I did have a little bit of difficulty locating the place where I was to stay. It was another thirty-five miles south of Atlanta, in a small town called Peachtree City.

And I couldn't see a thing in the pitch-black night. Peachtree was not at all lit up like Atlanta.

Having driven straight through, I was exhausted when I got there. I was very happy to find the place and finally sleep.

I got up the next morning and saw the beautiful place that is Peachtree City. It is probably one of the most ideal suburbs in the United States.

The town is interconnected with pathways for golf-carts. So, you can use a golf-cart to go anywhere at all there. The cart trails go underneath the adjacent roads, to avoid other traffic. With the trails bypassing the roads, you don't have to worry about crossing streets and things like this. Such a beautiful and hospitable suburb. This was the place Delta had picked for me, and they paid for it, as well.

Delta, in addition to the great housing, paid me a food allowance, and they even paid me mileage back and forth to the job site. So, I'd never had that good of a deal before in my life.

Delta, they really welcomed me into the family there.

It was also really a shock when I learned two of the guys I would be working with – they were premier and recognized in the development of networked flight schedules. Delta managed to have two such highly regarded programmers, Cleaver Randolph, and Jim Brown. They had thirty and thirty-five years respectively in the field, and they were each very good at their jobs. Delta could have been completely fine with either one of them.

Not only that, the methods in which they developed flight schedules had become the standard. These methods were copied and modeled throughout the industry.

I was told that Cleaver and Jim were getting overloaded in their work, and I was supposed to take this pressure off them, and I was, of course, tickled to death to do it.

One of the issues, for Delta at least, was that neither Cleaver nor Jim had written any description of what they were doing with their software. There was no documentation of any kind.

The manager in our department knew close to zero about the schedule development Cleaver and Jim were doing. This is the first time I've ever gone to a job where the boss was unable to describe what the job was, and what I was supposed to do.

I'll give you more about that as we go on.

It was a wild and an unusual way of working.

However, there were other things on my plate that I needed to handle.

I had made advance arrangements to contact a urologist, and with this I started the process of taking care of my cancer. I was so lucky that there was such good quality of care down there. The urologist was Dr. Clark at the Emory clinic. He happened to be right next door to the Center for Disease Control down in Atlanta.

That's who began giving me such great medical care, and he is probably the reason why I'm still living! Dr. Clark took me under his wing, and he had me on the operating table [*laughs*] within a few weeks' time.

He was extremely cordial, and an expert oncological urologist. I remember the date of surgery. It was the twentieth of May 1999.

Of course, I had no way of knowing what was gonna happen with the outcome of my surgery.

So, when I did wake up after the surgery, the doctor was standing there looking at me with a smile and I realized the crisis had passed and I had missed the whole thing! [*Laughs.*]

They let me know there was a small complication, that a vessel was almost severed in the surgery, though it had been resolved. Though, during the procedure, I had taken a lot of extra blood. As a result, the staff did observe me for a time to be sure the complication was indeed resolved. They had another doctor – a vascular surgeon – look at me, and I was finally given the okay. I had made it out of the woods!

I was free, I went home, and I was so happy that it was all over, and it had gone so well!

Dr. Clark said it had indeed been an aggressive cancer. He said he noticed during the surgery that around the tissue he was removing, cancer had also already started to spread to the surrounding tissues. Dr. Clark had to just take a bit more of the tissue, so it was no big deal for him.

On the third day after the surgery, when I was in the shower, suddenly, I looked at my left leg and it was completely swollen from the hip all the way down to the sole of my foot. I went back to the doctor and asked, "Can you folks do something about this swelling?"

I think it was Dr. Sam, the vascular surgeon – after he had determined that nothing had gone wrong with the surgery. He said, "I don't know that we *can* do anything about that."

I thought about it, and I said, "I think I can take it down if you'll allow me to walk," but they wouldn't allow me to walk yet – it was too soon after the surgery. I wasn't allowed any activity standing upright for long periods.

The doctor said to wait two more weeks, that any walking prior to that could injure the surgery site and create internal bleeding. I agreed to wait.

After the two weeks, I started walking on the cart trails near my place. I walked each day five miles.

The weather there is so humid and warm, I would

perspire like crazy. And I was hoping that this perspiration going through my skin would carry the extra fluid out and make the swelling go down in my left leg and, you know, it worked!

I had gotten rid of the swelling without having to go through additional surgery.

Things were fine for a while. There was an additional – minor – surgery, but it was nothing serious.

A month and a half after the cancer surgery, my free PSA level – the indicator for the presence of cancer – was climbing.

Dr. Clark saw me at this point and said, "We've gotta do something before the free PSA reading is too high and we can't save you anymore."

So, they scheduled me for seven weeks of daily x-rays and MRIs. They examined me from head to toe to see if the cancer had spread. Of course, I didn't know why they were scanning me so much.

It was determined that they would have to irradiate some areas to kill the leftover cancer cells to prevent further spread.

And I asked Dr. Lawrence, who oversaw the radiation therapy, "How do you know where to irradiate?"

He responded, "Well, we just go across the site where the operation was."

"Is there any way to prepare for this radiation therapy?" I asked him.

The doctor said they didn't know any special preparation, but that sometimes fatigue was a problem after treatments.

I just thought to myself, *I'll just get an extra hour of sleep for about a week before surgery*. And, lo and behold, that turned out to be a big boost for me! I went into the radiation treatment, and I would get up at five in the morning, go into the radiation therapy machine, treatment would start at seven in the morning, and for two hours, I was getting x-rayed.

Then, at about nine in the morning, I would jump in the car and drive into Delta and work from nine until five pm.

I was taken aback to hear my dad say this…
David: *Oh, seriously! Nothing keeps you from work, does it!*
Allen: *Yep, eight hours daily, and forty hours a week, but I found out I had no reserve. If I tried to work another half an hour, I would crash.*
David: *I should say so!*

I had just enough strength to make it through forty hours at Delta a week.

I discovered other people didn't have the same ability to just jump in their cars and go to work after their cancer treatments.

I would see the same people waiting with me each day at the clinic. And I remember seeing another couple – the wife was having a similar therapy as I was. I saw her break down, just from fatigue and the emotional cost of dealing with this catastrophic illness.

This lady reached her emotional limit in the waiting room, a few seats away from me, and was wailing and crying.

David: Having worked with cancer patients, I responded, "Yeah, they're very fragile, cancer patients – they can be emotional."

So, that extra sleep that I got before the whole therapy started, and this was enough to give me the strength to make it to the seven weeks. If it had been *eight* weeks, I might've been in a state like that poor woman.

I think too that the distraction of being at work helped me to not think too much about what was going on with my body.

Much later, I happened to have a recurrence of the cancer after twenty-two years. It was resolved too with therapy, and I've been paying attention to my free PSA levels since then.

Despite all these intrigues, cancers, and surgeries, I did manage to have a pretty good time down in Atlanta.

The management at Delta treated me well, I think better than I had ever been treated in any place before. They were very nice and accommodating to me as I was working so hard – at least in the beginning.

One thing, however, is that they could have given me time off, especially in the face of my cancer. I guess I should have advocated for myself more and that would have meant more time off, of course.

David: I could not believe what I was hearing... I've never heard of anybody working through that type of cancer radiation therapy before. I don't know, I guess the patients I see at the hospital probably work. I don't generally ask those types of questions when I scan or x-ray them. I don't say to patients, "Hey, are you going to work after this?"

There were two other things going on at that time too. I had taken my mother, Alice, and picked her up from her place in Florida, her rental home. I took her up to Paoli where she would live with Joan. This created issues with my sister Carol's kids, who wanted my mom to live with them. Alice and Joan also had issues and didn't get along well, causing all kinds of drama.

David: *I knew dad's mom could be difficult. I said: She wanted you only to take care of her, right?*

That's true, she wanted to be with me. Period. I just couldn't do that at the time. I had so much on my plate with cancer!

Unfortunately, due to her declining mental condition, she was having increasing issues. She, of course, wanted to be independent, but couldn't be trusted to not leave food on the stove, or similar things that could be hazardous.

In dealing with a parent as they age, it's a tightrope walk to allow them independence as much as possible and to be a support for them when they need help, as well.

She was acting out in ways, though, too. One day, she calls the police on Joan, saying that she's being abused.

A social worker was brought in because of the call. The social worker walked into the room and asked my mom, "Where's the evidence of your abuse? Can you show us?"

And she didn't have any, so the social worker also then said, "It's a penalty for making a false report."

Alice had to back off at that point from her claim of abuse.

She stayed a bit longer with Joan and then went from one care home to another, down near me, getting kicked out for her behavior often. Alice would hallucinate, also she'd pull out her IVs, and I would get calls at three a.m. that she was acting up, and I would have to come and help her.

It was especially difficult because she could seem lucid at times when she was talking about her medicine and how it was affecting her. So, a doctor, hearing this, how she was so affected, would lower the dose of some important medicine. Then I would get another call at three a.m., when she would act loopy without adequate medicine to keep her calm. [*Sighs.*] It was so tough caring for Alice during these years.

My mom had high medical bills which ate up all her money. In the end, there was no money at all. I didn't want my sister Carol's children to get nothing, so I gave them seven thousand dollars of my own money. This, however, was seen as a paltry amount by some in our family and some litigation resulted, unfortunately. Nothing ended up happening with the litigation, since there was no money that I was hiding.

All this drama prevented me from finishing a PhD program. I was paying for this program but couldn't do any work toward finishing my degree. This was at the University of Cincinnati and was distance learning.

Getting back to what the work at Delta was like.

Remember the programmers, Cleaver and Jim, who created the schedule system? They didn't make any written description of what they were doing.

I was working very differently. Delta would give me a little programming assignment, and I would go and do that job, and then write up a status report each week on what I did.

Management, they would then learn through my report how the scheduling worked by reading about all the processes of the schedule programming.

Maybe this reporting to management was the real reason for my presence at Delta. I didn't understand this until much later, unfortunately, that I was providing a roadmap to undermine the other, established programmers.

In an additional assignment, I would take another little part and I'd write that up in a report, as well. It was becoming obvious at weekly meetings that I was doing a lot of work. What I wasn't doing was anything directly with the two guys, Cleaver and Jim, who were undertaking so much more than I was, and I wasn't learning from them at all. I was just taking a piece of this and a piece of that. It felt like a waste of my time, in that sense.

Delta finally decided to buy a whole suite of schedule-editing software, which was the flagship of the entire industry. This suite of programs was made by American Airlines, which had a subsidiary called Sabre that wrote an editor for their flight schedule. It was an amazing and robust package of software. I mean, it could change flight times, places, and all user inputs on the fly. It was streamlined and worked seamlessly. That's why we all use it now – it's a great package!

These were, of course, just the kinds of things that Cleaver and Jim Brown were doing, but now access to all the inner workings of the software had been provided by me. It didn't feel good when I realized that.

David: I could see Delta's plan and confirmed... Oh, so they cut them outta the equation.

Not only that, but the new Sabre reservation suite was on the Unix operating system. So, they got off Windows too. Delta did that to axe Cleave and Jim. They cut them completely out of the situation after purchasing Sabre.

Well, in their defense, those guys were only trying to protect their own interests by protecting their knowledge. It's called gatekeeping. So, if Delta wanted anything done, they would have to come to Cleaver and Jim – they were the only ones working on that software. That had worked fine until Delta got fed up, and then hired me to document aspects of the inner workings of their program. And that gave Delta enough information to go with another package and get rid of them. Delta got tired of waiting for Cleaver and Jim to add this feature or that feature, and they didn't like the way they operated like a black box. Delta wanted more control of the whole environment of the schedule deployment. Delta, they certainly got what they wanted. It resulted in them saving a lot of money. It was shrewd of them! It didn't feel good to me, though I can see why they did it. Delta ended up hiring talent from outside the U.S., a programmer from China who was talented in assembler

ALLEN and DAVID GLINIEWICZ

language, and they hired Java programmers, as well.

The last thing – the thing that I'm most proud of in my work at Delta – was that I coordinated the automatic exchange of flight schedules between Delta and its business partners around the world. I don't remember the exact number of partners. There were thirty-three or thirty-eight, which all needed to be integrated.

One at a time, I went through these countries' flight schedule data, getting all these ready to be integrated. Eventually, I got all the airline partners' schedules so that they automatically transmitted and networked when they updated, to keep them current throughout the partner network.

Occasionally, somebody's computer would break down, and I'd have to do the file transfer protocol for that flight schedule myself, to get everything integrated. It was a huge task, and it was only me at this point doing the work. Meanwhile, Delta was laying off everybody. [*Laughs.*] Well, after a year, I became a regular Delta employee at Delta Technology rather than a consulting contractor. I stayed there five years, and in what would be my final year there, the amount of work they were giving us skyrocketed! We could not go five minutes without getting another job to do.

The boss would come over and say, "Here, there's nobody who can do this."

Of course, it was because they had laid everyone off.

More and more often we would get a little visit from the manager. We would hear a nonchalant voice. "Can you do this? I know you are already busy. Squeeze this in too."

Here's an example of how bad it got for me in my department at Delta.

There was a period where we needed to translate online scheduling menus into the French language – this was for our partner in France. Of course, by this time there was no one else on staff to do these many tasks. Nearly all the staff were let go at this point, leaving the barest of a skeleton crew. What I ended up doing, since I was the only one left to do the translation, was using free online translators to process all our website documents.

We all know how bad online translators can be. How I was able to get better translations was by translating the text to the new language, and then translating it back into English. I then checked to see if the language made any sense in English. If what I ended up with was garbage, then I tried to rephrase my document until it made sense when it came back into the original English from the round trip.

A quick example – during the work on the French Delta partner website, we were translating on the portal. I could not use the word "data" and have it translated into French. It just turned into garbage. If I used the word "information" instead, then that was fine, and was seamlessly translated into French and back. The abusive increase in workload became worse. Delta gave us pagers. At first, pagers were optional, but later we were on call twenty-four hours, and then it eventually included weekends. And then they finally got a new CEO at Delta. And this guy was incompetent, as far as I can tell. The only prior experience the new guy had was running an airline, and he put it in bankruptcy. [*Laughs.*] This now-bankrupt other airline was only one-fifth the size of Delta.

The work environment there just got so intolerable, I ended up leaving Delta in February of 2005. I had a friend that stayed and worked a little longer. I soon found that it got even worse. I heard that they had women pass out on the job. I think there were three of them who collapsed at their desks, just fainted, fell over at their desks!

Another employee had an appointment with the doctor and the boss wouldn't let her off work long enough to go to the appointment. She reported the manager to HR, and that manager was let go as a result.

David: This was the beginning of the transition back to Texas for my dad. The extremely lean staff at Delta had created an environment that would have run him to the ground, quite literally.

I was preparing to go to live with my girlfriend Gloria at her place in Texas, a little town called Brookshire.

Before I could go, I had to get rid of my condo near Atlanta in Dunwoody. I got the condo when I was hired as full-time staff at Delta.

I was working, trying to fix it up so that I could rent it out for an income. I was not prepared for being a long-distance landlord and property manager, and all the "fun" that went along with that.

There was a problem, and I didn't realize it prior to me moving. There was a creaking of the floors, and it bothered the people downstairs. I guess the new tenants were jumping around in the condo more energetically than I was. It was apparently so loud the downstairs residents had to put earphones on to be able to hear a TV.

There was concrete between the first and second floors. My place was on the second floor.

David: Let me just say here that I don't think there was any issue with sound going through concrete. Even if the concrete was cracked, it should not have had sound getting through it. There must have been something structural happening between the floors of the units to have that much noise happening.

Every time somebody would walk across it, it would creak like mad. And so, I asked the management, "Do you know how long it would take to fix this thing?"

The condo property manager said it would be about four days' work. However, it would take about thirty days for them to present this to the condo association and then vote on it.

David: Since the work was on structural concrete, Allen would not be able to do it himself. I did not catch this during the actual interview with my dad, however.

In the meantime, well, I thought I could handle that, since I was just working on the place myself. I was getting the place in shape to be able to rent it again. And then I realized, while we were painting, that we should never have tried to do that paint before the concrete work because, when the actual concrete work started, it would go on for about three months, not at all the four days that I was told.

This long delay in the fixing of my unit also meant I had to carry the load and pay the mortgage of the unoccupied place. I ran my savings out carrying that expense, all due to the slow action of the condo association and their workers.

At this point, I was in Brookshire and sweating the issues of the extra expenses the condo construction was causing.

Brookshire
and Katy, Texas

Allen

I came back west to Texas with Gloria. We lived together in Brookshire and later in Katy, Texas.

So, it was tough in Brookshire in the beginning, unfortunately, I think mainly due to my condo worries.

Brookshire is about thirty miles straight west of Houston on the Katy Freeway, a straight shot. I lived there with Gloria, and shortly after I came there, Gloria's daughter joined us, as well.

I handled pretty much all the outside things that had to be done around the house. We had a little over two acres of ground which, of course, needed regular maintenance. The toughest job there was keeping the front pasture mowed. That was about a square acre, there.

I ran the lawnmower, a little five-horsepower thing, until it just wore its transmission completely out. [*Laughs*.] By the time we were ready to leave the place, the lawnmower just couldn't go anymore.

We did a lot of things. If you can imagine all the lawn and garden maintenance on an acre, and that was just the front. The backyard added another acre for us. I can see why people in retirement get a low-maintenance place to live. This ranch certainly wasn't that.

So, there was a lot to do. And there was a guesthouse on the property that was about 2,500 square feet. That required some attention too.

We had all the wildlife to contend with in Texas too, with tarantulas and everything else, including copperhead snakes! Gloria wasn't too shy about taking the copperhead snakes and putting them down. [*Laughs.*]

We had a 700-acre farm next to us, where a friendly farmer and his wife lived. Our neighbors helped us – they were good friends. The people across the way were friendly, also. It was the Indian Oaks section of Brookshire, and it was an extremely rural place. When we finally left, in 2012, we were ready for it! *More* than ready to get out of there. The upkeep did not agree with us well.

But I – luckily – eventually convinced Gloria to move. She had been attached to the place.

Gloria had some miniature horses at the ranch. She loved them and had won some medals with these beautiful animals. But taking care of them was just exhausting for Gloria, and it was financially draining too. So, I convinced her, before we could think about moving, we really needed to find a home for the horses. So, that was handled too. Homes were found for them in the area. I'm sure it was hard for Gloria to part with them, but we worked it out, and were closer to being able to move.

Then we focused back inside the ranch and took care of some maintenance issues to get the place ready for sale. We replaced the water treatment system, which is something you need if you live in Texas on a ranch.

That was pretty much the end of the time we spent in Brookshire.

Meanwhile, we had begun making frequent trips into Houston. I was already singing in the choir weekly, in a cultural district where there were theaters, parks, and museums.

We sang every Monday night. Our group did very well and were even a bit of a financial success. The choir had a decent following in Houston, and I just felt great being part of the group.

Our group had grown to 150 members. Many of them were professionals and graduate students from the local universities, even cantors from synagogues and other churches around. So, Gloria and I were a part of this cultural community and thriving!

Additionally, we attended regular meditation sessions, and eventually became strongly affiliated with the Edgar Cayce group. I'll talk about this later, also, since it's a bit unconventional. He is known as the father of holistic medicine.

I was getting great medical treatment by a local doctor and the VA and had established contacts for medical care.

While still in Brookshire, just before moving, we were befriended by a special little resident who came into our lives. We were visited by a little cat, black and white. Gloria called the feline visitor Bema. And we soon discovered why she was so friendly. She… [*Laughs.*] After a short while, she delivered five little kittens.

The first one born was a black-and-white tomcat named Boots, with black-and-white hind legs. And then there were three greys, all with white socks. And then the last one was all black, and we called her Silky – Silky Sue. She was a wonderful cat.

Bema was a brilliant mom. She trained her little kittens and she taught 'em all how to climb trees. [*Laughs.*] I go outside one day, and here they're all up in the trees. Some of 'em were twelve feet or more off the ground.

Shortly after that, the mother departed and left us with the kittens. We were able to find good homes for the three gray cats, and we kept Boots and Silky.

When we moved to the other house in Katy, Boots didn't want to come. He was basically an outside cat.

Boots would hang out and stalk the backyard of our place. He was so stealthy, so hidden, I didn't realize he was hiding out in the backyard all that time. He just wanted to be out there, and I wasn't feeding him. Boots ended up taking off.

He was befriended by someone else. Much later, I saw him. He had eventually gone all the way to the other side of Katy. Boots, being Boots… He also wandered away from the first family who took him in, and then stayed with a family of migrant workers who lived nearby. Maybe they had better food there.

It was during this time that we moved to Katy.

Gloria's daughter, Lia, had found a nice house in Katy that was specially designed for handicapped usage. The floors were all the same level, and it was a beautifully made place. The whole house was elevated above the floodplain. The surrounding houses would easily become flooded, with the expansive flat ground of the surrounding territory, but not this place.

The area had once been used to grow rice, so the whole terrain was flat. Years of rice farming had made the ground itself firm and packed together. When a flood came – which was often, with any type of continued rain – the whole area would become flooded. However, our house was high enough, thanks to the original builder of the place, that it would never be flooded. My story with the cats now continues…

Allen: I felt sorry, but I didn't get along with Boots well at all. Silky, however, was a wonderful cat. Her surprising manner was unique for a cat. Silky Sue was well-behaved and, more than that, was really like a person, and a friend.

Silky [*laughs*] would eat food from my bowl! Whatever I was having, whether it be cereal or wine at night, it didn't matter, she wanted some too! I'd take a few flakes of cereal each morning and put it on the side for Silky. And she'd sit there and eat the bran flakes. But she didn't like other types of cereal, with odd little shapes – she didn't care for that.

She would sit in my lap and watch television. [*Laughs.*] Especially, she was very interested when bird shows came on the Nature channel. Silky would walk up to the screen, and she would eventually realize that there wasn't a real bird there. She pawed the screen and would have an ah-ha moment, like, "Oh, these are just pictures."

And then she'd come back and sit in my lap. [*Laughs.*]

I swear that cat could almost read my mind.

Silky was also very much a night cat. She liked to get some food at about three in the morning. So, between one and three, she would come over and wake me up, though there would already be food in her dish each night. Silky would not eat what was in her bowl until I walked over there and shined the flashlight on it. [*Laughs.*] When I did that, she knew it was okay to eat. This ritual continued every night there for a long time.

Besides me, Gloria, and the cat, there were many other things I had with me in the house...

Being a lover of books, I had many. In Katy, I had a place for all of my collection.

I'd set up my desk and stuff. I almost had a regular office there, with room enough for all my books and materials in one of the spare rooms. It worked out very well. We were happy. This was also where I wrote my first book.

We were also thankful to be driving a shorter distance from Katy than we were from Brookshire for all the trips we made into Houston.

Gloria and I attended meetings at the Edgar Cayce group. We enjoyed 'em a lot. They were meetings with friends and fellow choir members. We were about ten to fifteen minutes from where the gatherings were held, so it was great to be so close.

These sessions were focused on the book that Cayce

had written, *In Search of God*. This book is a collection of religious writings, and at the meetings we would go through sections and discuss them. Edgar Cayce was quite spiritual. Even though he was famous for his work in medicine, the book which we were studying was a spiritual text.

As members of the Edgar Cayce group, we got access to all the readings and materials. There are like fourteen thousand different writings on all types of diseases, and it's just amazing that he was essentially uneducated at any kind of high level, and yet he was 90% accurate in diagnosing all kinds of diseases.

He has descriptions of his special preparations, and descriptions of materials and their use. He had very specific instructions, particularly for things like iodine – these were special types of iodine and other solutions that were indicated for various medical treatments.

It was almost as if somebody from the future was dictating to him to allow Cayce to grasp these medical processes without having learned them. He also had sort of a nickname, The Sleeping Prophet.

Cayce was telepathic and was able to be located far away – in France, for example – and still speak and dictate to a remote secretary thousands of miles away in the U.S. The secretary recorded and typed up his remarks, and this was the way in which so many entries could be contributed to Cayce's huge body of work.

Part of his work is a physician's reference. I purchased one. It deals with different medical conditions and suggests remedies for them. But I wanna warn somebody who's considering using it as some kind of treatment guide, that you must look hard at this volume and know that Cayce's diagnoses and processes of treatment were based on the specific individuals he treated. You must have some discretion to figure out if Cayce's treatment is appropriate for a situation outside of his specific, intended use.

So, that's a word of caution in reading Cayce's work. The work is dated, also, because Edgar Cayce died some time ago, in 1945, and you know, progress marches on.

David: We can maybe note that my dad possibly saw Cayce as a prototype and template for his own spiritual journey, one of melding the scientific and spiritual.

Despite all these cautions regarding Cayce's work, he is a compelling individual.

We attended meetings on Saturday mornings for the Cayce group. Also, I would have breakfast with a bunch of other retired engineers, and some who weren't yet, but would soon be retired. They were still working at aerospace and other technological companies around, down in the heart of Houston.

This group were all science fiction buffs, like me. These guys knew most sci-fi movies. They had all seen them many times over. [*Laughs.*] And many of these guys had their PhDs already. So, they were also very knowledgeable. In fact, one of the guys, Hal Jackson, celebrated his fiftieth year at NASA, and is still teaching astronauts at Johnson Space Center.

Hal's wife was a doctor – Dr. Janice Schwarz, a dermatologist. She treated me for a melanoma. I was so lucky to have such easy access to medical treatment even in my group of friends.

The group I sang with was affiliated with the United Nations, and called the International Voices of Houston, and they are still going these days. And I still have communication with the people, members of that choir. I was with them for nine years and did a lot of wonderful concerts.

Our official schedule was to sing two concerts, originally – a Christmas concert and a spring one. In time, we added a third concert in summer. You can find them on YouTube at International Voices of Houston.

During the pandemic, the choir did independent recordings, which were then edited together for a combined performance as a sort of virtual choir, all merged together into one song. It was a novel way to overcome not being able to get together during the quarantine. I do prefer the sound of a full, live choir, though.

David: *One last question for the discussion of Houston, Texas, and events there. You were a longtime member of the Jung Center. Can you describe what the Jung Center is, and what the philosophies that are found there are based? I do know it was founded by Carl Jung, the famous psychiatrist who was mentored by Sigmund Freud. People may not know about him, and I think it was a huge influence on you, this place.*

Oh, yeah, it was. The Jung Center is an interesting place, located in Houston. The center teaches Jung's analytical psychology, which he pioneered.

Jung's understanding of the collective unconscious is the cornerstone of his work. It provides a framework that enables us to find a way of dealing with the unconscious. Jung's further methods for segmentation of the psyche, psychological types, all the other shadow-selves we have within us, the anima and animus, and the use of symbolism interpretation, these are all terms which Jung provides to give us this framework.

The center has a very broad base. They offer a lot of different schools and courses. These build upon the concepts of Jung's theories and philosophies. The center offers dream and body movement workshops, and other things, like lectures, are given there.

I was involved in the advanced dance group, called the Movement Group, run by Carolyn Faye, who was president of the Jung Center for many years, and one of the major contributors there. And she had credentials as a dance therapist and would teach us body movements to link to our unconscious. We would learn to use dance and movement to decode the various symbolisms we encountered in dreams and meditations. I was involved in the dance group for probably three or four years. And I discussed this somewhat in my first book, entitled *It Clicks*.

As for how long I was at the center, I started attending in October of 1970.

In the beginning, I was just attending monthly lectures, and then eventually started taking classes and workshops. As time went on, I ended up taking classes in just about everything I could think of in their offerings. I attended several of their summer conferences. These had nationally or internationally known experts who would teach a week of classes in a lecture series at what used to be called the

Compassionate Father's Retreat House.

Since then, they've sold this property, and the center stopped having conferences in 1982 or 83.

There were a staggering number of offerings at the center – even classes in poetry, yoga, sculpture, and of course dance movement.

I also took classes in understanding symbolism from Evelyn Gibson. She drew inspiration for a lot of her work in the class from the book *The Symbolic Quest* by Edward Whitmont.

I really liked the way she presented her classes, and I learned a lot about the process of active imagination from her.

David: *Oh yeah, that was another one of my questions. I remember you talking about active imagination when I was growing up. Can you describe the process of active imagination, what it is, and how it works?*

Boy, well – it's sort of the Jungian version of what you would call "free association" in the Freudian terminology. And when you try to use active imagination, you open yourself to the understanding of the symbolic images from the unconscious and try to use this understanding to decode the messages of these symbols.

It's so flexible, this method, that it's literally a whole field of looking at imagination. And I got so practiced with this method that working with Jonathan, my psychologist and friend, I can go into a deep meditation in probably three minutes.

And the nice thing about active imagination is that it can be used to do movement, and then you can ask questions in your mind telepathically and get answers as to the meaning of dream symbols through the means of the different movements.

That's one of the main ways we use active imagination – through movement, as a way to interpret dreams. And we found that made it pretty evident that if you go into this light meditative state and take the shape and posture of images, people, and figures in the dreams, you pick up on the emotional feelings those figures represent.

It's a great help to understand the dreams, using your body as a way to decode the symbols. And, of course, a big advantage of it is that you can stop and ask questions and get answers to the questions, these being provided directly from the unconscious.

I've learned a lot of these meditation practices, and I presented these in my first book, as well. These methods came from active imagination. Some of the descriptions and big discoveries, for me, anyway – it meant so much to me, this training. It changed my life!

I guess not the least of these changes was the fact that contact with God was made in a session of active imagination. I was in a dialogue with God, and I felt that he didn't have an ego, because it became obvious from some of the ways that He spoke to me.

With this understanding, I then focused a tremendous amount of the work that I was doing on the overcoming of my own ego, to minimize this shortcoming. And this experience explained a great many things to me – the interface of communication with God, and the difficulties ego presents to us as humans.

David: Would you say that dance precluded language? And, if I'm understanding right, the actual posture of a character, or a diagram of a pose, holds within it the symbolic message, and this message is in the essence of the posture. And this essence and message of the pose is different than the words we might use to describe the stance. It holds power *placing yourself in the pose, and a message is then transmitted to us.*

The emotional content of it. Yeah, you can feel the emotions when you take the pose.

David: I couldn't help but have the music video for Madonna's dance song "Vogue" flash in my mind when my dad was saying this! I wanted to blurt out, "Vogue!" but I thought it might spoil the moment, so I kept that to myself just then. I did continue, however, with a more appropriate thought I had at that same moment...though I was still picturing Allen voguing...

Language and the characters we use for writing... these grew from dance, right?

So, for instance, a question mark. If we were to put our body into this position – it's a symbol portraying uncertainty or the need for more information... of searching within ourselves for something. If a person emulates that gesture, their figure is hunched over, and thus contemplating themselves –think of the phrase "contemplating your navel."

So, in that posture, we would feel questioning, right? That's the sort of feeling we get from being hunched over. And the opposite type of symbol, I guess, would be shown in taking the position of an exclamation point, where you're upright and sort of extending upward vertically rather than hunching over.

David: *So, these two contrasting examples… If you were to see them in a dream… You see a hunched-over man. If you put yourself in that posture, you would feel questioning, and just the opposite with the energized and upright position of the exclamation point. Is that sort of a summary of working with these symbols and how they might bring a feeling when doing these poses?*

Sure, that may be true, but you must remember – one thing I discovered with active imagination is that you must be careful. And I emphasize that because it is so flexible that there are a lot of different ways you can read a symbol, and it just depends on the individual and the symbol, the emotional state of the interpreter, also the depth of the meditative state at the time. It's all subjective. I've had cases where exactly, and I do mean exactly, the same symbol occurred in two different dreams and meant two totally different things. So, you must ask the questions to find out the meaning and the context.

I remember an example that might help describe the process a bit. In the epilogue of my book, I describe symbols that I encountered. This is one of the pivotal meditations that I had, where I went to my own church. And this was the sort of…prompt of the meditation – it was to come and explore a church which was your very own. And the priest led me to a room below, down some stairs off to the right of the altar and threw back the lid of this ornate chest that was there. Inside were gems the size of the palm of my hand.

And I asked the question, "What am I going to do

with these? I can't eat them, and I certainly wouldn't wear them."

And the answer came back from the priest, "You can give them away."

And it turned out to be very important, because later, at the end of the meditation, he brought me up to the altar, and monks were there distributing communion. The priest indicated to me that I should distribute communion too.

And I said, "All right, but all I have are these gems, a pocketful of them." So, I didn't have any wine to offer. My line was all women, and I put a gem in the hand of each woman, and when the gem touched each lady's hand, it would turn into a deep-red rose. With each woman in the line, the gem would either become one or four roses, or a small bunch of them, or sometimes a whole stream of roses right up to a woman's shoulder.

And I gave them away this way. All the women were satisfied with what I had given them.

Then, as I was departing from the church, walking away down the aisle, I thought, and I asked a last question just then, "What makes the difference in the number of roses on the women's hands?"

And the answer came back, "It's what each woman expected."

David: It sounds like you got a lot of information from that session. Could this be related to another type of dream practice? Are you familiar with lucid dreaming, or do you practice that at all?

I've had a few lucid dreams. Very few, but I have had some, yeah. Where you are in a dream and realize that you're dreaming and working consciously within to shape the dream with your will. Lucid dreaming is different from the process of active imagination, though.

I can see that there's sort of similarities to active imagination. With active imagination, because it's meditation and not a sleeping state, you can engage and double-check what the meaning is, or what the message is, that you're supposed to be gaining from the interaction. And that, perhaps, is the difference to lucid dreaming – in a dream, we are taken on a journey, but a dream is less of a conversation.

In active imagination, you must use discernment and maybe double-check things. The depth of the meditation is so slight that you can pull yourself out of it by asking a question. It's a light form of meditation.

If you have an additional question – maybe, you don't understand the answer that is presented. You could also have other reservations and you can voice those, and you'll get answers in this case too. You see, it's like the first question I asked when I found the gems, "What am I going to do with these?"

I had been presented with an opportunity to do this or that, but I really didn't have any idea what I might do until I received some more direction. After having asked, what the priest then offered me was another alternative I hadn't considered. This guidance came from God, of course.

David: *What's the reason for the journaling of dreams? Is this so you could go back and do an active imagination session with the symbolism from a particular dream, and get what was happening?*

Because I can't remember them, otherwise. If I don't write something down within a short time, it's gone. So, I do that because I have to, otherwise I can't handle it. But it's certainly possible to do an active imagination with a symbol you have written down. And, in fact, Dr. Ruth Fry, who was the director of the Jung Center while I was there… Dr. Fry was also my analyst. She said that you can always finish your dream.

Sometimes, while dreaming, you happen to wake up at an inopportune moment, and you can later finish a dream, if you'd like, based on your records of what you have written, or you can go into a dream and, at some point, take a different point of view than you had previously, and see what the dream does with the new focus.

Yes, you can certainly reenter it and go a divergent way or take a new path and make new choices. Ruth used to frequently make that suggestion to me about a given dream, to revisit and create a new outcome, or to finish something that was unresolved or unclear.

David: *Yeah, that's interesting. And this might be outside of the sphere of what we're talking about, but have you practiced, or have you encountered any type of astral travel outside of the body, anything like this?*

Oh, I think so. Yeah.

David: *Right. You sort of described things recently which would fit into that category, also.*

Yeah, I think, well, recently I was taken out this way not of my own accord, rather than something I initiated myself, which is typically what astral travel is. And when it happened recently, then I said, well, I want to find out what it's about, what it wants to show me.

So, I let it show me.

In other moments, I would get strong indications when faced with a choice or action. This is much different than traveling like we were talking about. So, sometimes I will get warnings from the unconscious – oh, don't do this, or don't do that.

I described a warning like this in my first book too. One time, I had a dream where I was walking along a dike, like the Dutch boy in the fairytale that comes over and finds a hole. He must plug the hole with his finger to keep the water from flowing out. In this dream I did that also…

David: *Sure, that's what you do when you see a hole in a dike, right?*

So, my hand is there, and I keep the water from flowing out. I felt that the water was strong and surging on the other side of the dike. And, finally, when I started concentrating on that, I started to take my hand out, and suddenly, I was in the violently turbulent ocean myself, on the ocean side of the dike, and floundering around, trying desperately to swim, to get out of there. I felt, at that point, that the unconscious was trying to drown me, just swamping me with water, with waves and spray, leaving me gasping for breath, for fear of the next wave.

And I finally stood there and said, in challenge, "You can silence me, but if you do and I'm dead, you lose my voice on this planet. I won't be able to speak."

And I opposed the ocean, at this point – which was, of course, the unconscious – is saying: You can take my life if you want to, but if you do, I'll be gone, and I won't be able to speak and to share what you want me to tell the world.

Suddenly, the storm went quiet. It was serene and calm after my challenge. The storming ocean didn't really want to kill me. It was only trying to frighten me.

David: *I guess you called its bluff.*

Yeah, you could say that. And I think it does happen, this kind of thing. I've heard when dealing with the unconscious this happens to almost everyone at some point in work with symbology. Everyone who ever attempts to understand the unconscious has this kind of confrontation, where they have to assert themselves or be lost.

The unconscious mind challenges you and demands of you as if saying, "Are you ready to lay your life on the line for this?"

And the unconscious wants you to see that it is important, and that it can also be dangerous. By working with the unconscious, you're not playing a game. You must take care in what you're doing and care about the outcome. It does challenge you to put your money where your mouth is, and to stand up for yourself when you need to.

David: *Would it be fair to say that the unconscious is important, and so are we, living our lives in this world, and we need each other, in a partnership, to move forward and to know our true potential, both are needed.*

Yes, I think so. I'll include a quote which I think is appropriate…

"The difference between a good life and a bad life is how well you walk through the fire."– Carl Jung

110

My previous example of these kinds of powerful images was when the unconscious scared me so badly while working at NASA, showing the destruction of the buildings by boulders the size of the structures themselves.

The symbols of that dream, they meant something else – budget cuts. If I would have thought it meant asteroids hitting the complex, that would have been a whole different outcome, and it would have been wrong, of course. You must really be ready to lay your life on the line in dealing with this stuff. It separates the men from the boys.

David: *Yeah. Well, I guess it's a catalyst for real growth.*

It challenges you in asking, Are you serious about this? If you really want to solve this issue, here is the answer, and you must figure out… the symbolism.

David: *In summary, we can take the symbols from dreams and meditate on them to unlock hidden meanings in the symbols. These symbols we can apply directly to our lives the moment we have them, though we have to figure out the true meaning. Right?*

I call meditation a spiritual conversation, with all the flexibility that this implies. It can start anywhere and go anywhere. So, dreaming, you have access to symbols from the spiritual world, and in meditation you can have a conversation about them, yes, but the vocabulary is far greater in meditation – you can end up lightyears away from where you started.

PART 2:

Through the Looking Glass

The Ethereal Summit

"You're mad, bonkers, completely off your head.
But I'll tell you a secret. All the best people are."
– Lewis Carroll, Alice in Wonderland

"Senility is just a convenient peg on which to hang
nonconformity."
– Frances, a resident in a nursing home
(Reported by Ram Dass, Conscious Aging)

David

Allen had ascended to the summit of the glass mountain. However, neither he nor anyone surrounding him knew that the actual summit was in another realm entirely.

This part of the journey which we are about to take with my dad is one that flies in the face of conventional spiritual practice, thought, and concepts, and it might get a little uncomfortable.

Spontaneous and metaphysical things, like telepathic communication, conversations with spirits, these are things that we normally would reserve for fairy tales, and these are what we need to call forth to meet Al where he now is.

Allen and I have hours of recorded dialogue and conversations from this period of great change.

Due to the ephemeral nature and the plastic state of Al's new awareness, I find it better to describe the events of this period as a narrative, a parable.

In telling Allen's other-worldly journey, I hope to share the power of Al's experiences, and to distill the value from it all in a way which is more attuned to magic, both dark and light, than my prose.

Perhaps I can better tell Allen's story in a fairy tale. I will reframe my dad as a mythic character and rename him, as in India. As we know, fairy tales have both positive and negative – good and evil are portrayed as part of our world, ephemeral or not.

In both worlds, on the summit and below, Allen deals with the threat of cancer. This tale will cast cancer as one of the players.

Al has nearly cut loose his tether to this world, though he keeps his orbit near enough to us on the ground. We will need to make a leap to meet him where he is now.

Let me help you now, and myself too!

I'm going to loosen our tether on my dad's heart that we all keep so tight – some of us tighter than others – with our mundaneness, with our worry, with our As the World Turns brand of drama, with our anger and fear of change. These bonds will soon all fall away.

When we fly kites in the U.S., and most of the world, the kite goes up in the air, the kite soars or does tricks, and then, after a time, it gets pulled back earthward – game over!

Kite-flying in India is a whole different thing entirely from what we normally do. In India, the kites' strings have ground glass on them, just enough to make them like sandpaper. The kite goes up, and maybe the neighbors' kite too. There is a battle and drama to kite-flying in India, to try to entangle your string with your neighbor's and break it, if you can manage it! If it does break, the kite is free to go where it will. Maybe you get the kite, maybe your neighbor, maybe it flies to the stratosphere, or Fiji.

You can find a beautiful description of kite flying in India in Paramahansa Yogananda's Autobiography of a Yogi.

If we are, indeed, one being, one heart and one spirit, some of us, our hearts happen to be hardened, in this collective. And in this combined heart and spirit, in this connectivity to all the other hearts as one synchronic pulse, then the heavy hearts, the burden they create, are they not the weight we feel as gravity tugging our own hearts down?

If our hardened hearts' weight decided not to be heavy, to drop away, and we let go our grudging hold, could then the suddenly unburdened, light hearts go where they might?

If we release our downward pull on a lightened heart, and it lofts to new heights, it is to our credit that we did this, we chose it!

Let's choose this, as if it's we who would fly because of our choice, as if it's we, ourselves, surveying the skies up so high, and we are ready to break the bonds of terra firma!

And, untethered, we go... to witness a mythic tale, now full of both darkness and light.

My dad, with a new name... a new face... a freed kite!

Remember, a kite goes where it may – high aloft, or mired in the mud, or perhaps both.

We now join Herac at the summit. This is where he had striven to be all his life – the apex of the glass mountain. This is not the end of Herac's journey, however. The summit offers another, more complex, path to explore. Into the ether we go!

This is an idyllic part of the story, in which Herac meets a luminary being and feels a profound love. Herac lives in two worlds during his adventures, on the summit and at his home in the mundane world. Herac struggles to maintain a presence in both worlds, not only because that is difficult, but also because people near him can be grasping and a burden, keeping Herac's mindset largely an earthbound one.

Herac suddenly found himself on the summit of the mountain upon which he had set his sights throughout his life.

What to do now? he thought.

In his advanced age, Herac was looking forward to study and to recounting his worldly accomplishments with friends and loved ones. He felt his rest was well-earned. Herac had prospered in his prior life, in the measured, rational, and competitive world, and rose high with his mighty intellect. He understood the underpinnings of the mundane world all too well.

Herac loved the stratagems the problems of the mundane world and what these offered his mind. He longed to engage in solving more lofty and challenging puzzles on the summit.

However, on the summit, no puzzles presented themselves to Herac – though the spirit realm also called a little more loudly to him than it had in his life far below, the pristine slopes of the glass mountain. Herac longed to engage his mind in working a problem. He felt his mental faculties becoming soft and flabby with the ease of life in retirement. Herac laughed to himself, "How funny it is that in my work life, I felt such a pull to the spirit realm and marveled in my visions, and these visions guided me so well.

"Now, in this ideal world, I'm in a place where I can relax in the spiritual, and I want nothing but to work a problem.

"Am I missing something? Is it through some fault of mine that this is where I am?

"I'm feeling so useless. I won't last too long this way." To stave off a sense of uncertainty, Herac would meditate with the goal of finding an answer to the predicament in which he found himself. Herac was intent on finding meaning for himself in a world where he was now a foreigner. At last, Herac had found a problem to which he could apply his skills of logic and deduction. The game was afoot!

Herac settled down and began his practice, as he had innumerable times. He quickly felt the dawning of his oneness with spirit. He thought he would meditate on his own faults as a goal for that session. Maybe some insight would help him…

It can never hurt to know one's faults, right? Herac thought to himself, as he settled his mind for meditation.

Soon, in the silent mindscape of meditation, Herac came upon a being…Sensing an ample, yet benevolent, figure present in his meditation, Herac asked the imposing figure, "Are you God?"

"Yeah, the big one!" the exceedingly tall figure

replied, with a surprising joviality.

Herac then laughed and laughed, because that was how *he* would have spoken if he were answering that same question. He couldn't believe that God had come to him at last!

Herac called this buoyant being Megalotypos, or MT, and was awed by his large stature, and even more by his presence.

Megalotypos had discerned Herac's way of talking, as if he were transparent, and read his mind with only a moment's effort. Herac was in awe and knew that this must be his god because he knew him intimately. His manner and humor were present in all Megalotypos said. The being showed Herac the creation of his own soul in a mindscape vision. It was such a powerful experience that Herac wept openly, fell to his knees, and grasped Megalotypos by the legs. Herac knew with even more certainty this was his god, his creator, who had forged his very soul. *And of what material is my soul composed*? Herac wondered, and asked Megalotypos. Megalotypos said that it was from his own self that he gave the base from which to then weave the soul, heart, and being of Herac.

MT's sense of humor was what really was the hook for Herac. It was completely disarming to him.

During their meeting, Herac and MT had conversations, sharing a stream of thoughts and mindscapes to express themselves wordlessly

After the glow of the visit from MT had left him, Herac used the new wordless and instantaneous path of communication and inquired of MT about his weaknesses. Herac had been dazzled by the presence of MT, and he had forgotten to ask.

Herac was then given a dream by MT, a dream in which he was shown his weaknesses, and he understood why his weaknesses had been presented in this way, in his disarmed dream-mind.

As with any of us, seeing our own faults is something we may have a great amount of trouble doing. When they are illustrated and presented in a dream, they are much easier, possibly, to accept.

Our faults are also something deeply rooted, inextricably so, perhaps, and yet we can pretend they are not there. There can also be a lot of self-judgement and shame locked away in these parts of ourselves. We might like to tell ourselves a story about our weaknesses, of how they're justified, and we keep them going and growing this way.

When Herac saw his own faults, he was humbled, and it was a shock to his core to see these laid out with such matter-of-factness. Herac could also see how his faults had played out in his life below the summit. The euphoria Herac had felt during his meeting with MT had been replaced by shame and the regret of having been influenced by his now-revealed faults, which had caused him to harm people he loved, and himself.

After the sting of the dream of Herac's faults had eased and had a chance to marinate in him, MT spoke to Herac, again in the very idiom he himself used, Herac's own humor shining through in Megalotypos' jokes and smile. Herac felt an ease and acceptance of his own faults and, more importantly, MT's acceptance, as well. He felt truly seen and stripped bare in the eyes of his god, and everything was okay. There was no judgment, no purgatory or damnation, only sudden ease. A sense of relief and peace had replaced the shame of only a moment earlier, and Herac felt a deep acceptance from MT. Herac and MT enjoyed an idyllic bond in the ethereal world. After the visit ended, however, Herac could not keep himself from sharing stories with his friends and family at home of his blissful contact with MT. The marvelous moment when Herac saw the creation of his own soul had left such an indelible mark on him…

Herac suddenly asked MT, on a whim, "Could I too create souls as you do?"

"Sure!" Herac had not expected such a quick and positive answer from MT. He had rather thought that this was something reserved for God, creating souls. Herac thought, *I must have been elevated in my being to be able to do such a thing!*

This period with MT was serene for Herac. He felt the glow of warm love from MT day and night. Herac, when he slept, felt that he was lying in MT's warm, open hands. There was not a moment during this time when Herac felt any distance or separation from MT.

When Herac had a conversation with his most trusted and loved friend, Ioanath, he also had a moment with MT…

"I love you, Ioanath!"

"I love you too, Herac."

And at the same moment, in Herac's mind, he heard, *I love you too, Herac.* This was in MT's familiar and ever-present voice. And there was nothing that Herac could not tell Ioanath, so Herac let Ioanath know that MT had also chimed in at their tender moment. Herac then spread the word to all those around him of the powerful experience of seeing the creation of his soul, and now too his recruitment and participation in this amazing process.

MT gave Herac jobs with increasing complexity and responsibility. The first job was to maintain the grounds of a park. Herac was underwhelmed with this task, and asked if he could solve important problems, like he did so well in the world below the summit. Herac was assured, with a warm smile, that MT could find other jobs for him.

It was then, after emerging from his meditation, that Herac noticed his eyes were impaired and he was fumbling to do the easiest of tasks.

"I will turn your face to alabaster
When you'll find your servant is your master
You'll be wrapped around my finger…"

– The Police, "Wrapped Around Your Finger"

Herac's vision was failing. Incremental degradation had been going on for a while. His eyes were now nearly robbed entirely of sight. Due to his dependance on his sight, Herac saw one healer after another for years, and this was a condition which was not well enough understood to afford any treatments. Herac was told by the learned healers and surgeons to accept that he would not be able to see one day.

The loss of Herac's sight had progressed further. He mentioned this to MT, and MT shared with Herac the cause of his blindness. His sightlessness was due to a collection of insects so small as to not be seen, and these fed on the linkages behind the eyes. Herac was told which potion would kill the minute insects – drops of sulfa in the eyes.

Herac then faithfully used the potion and had a degree of healing. Further use was prevented after this recovery by the healers who observed Herac. They were rigid, tethered to the earth types. In their concrete thinking, it was not an accepted form of treatment.

"Little bugs in the eyes, really?" they said. The healing of Herac's eyes halted and what filled in the space of the lack of sight were visions both divine and corrupted. All manner of divine inspirations and threats came to Herac. At first, Herac knew what was solid and what was ephemeral, yet day by day Herac's discernment of the mundane world was lost a bit more.

Herac was able to contact his father, who had passed away many years ago. Herac found that his dad, named Náftis, was in the spirit realm, just sitting in a darkened space. Herac let Náftis know that in the spirit realm, he could think of a place he would like to travel to, and he would be brought there instantly. The power of the mind was all that was necessary to travel anywhere he could visualize. Herac saw Náftis go off with his newfound freedom. Herac wondered how long Náftis had sat in silence and darkness.

Herac also later spoke to the reincarnation of Náftis. It was interesting, because in his life with Herac, Náftis had always wanted to be a healer, but his life situation did not allow it to be.

Herac found the young incarnation of Náftis, who was living, as Herac was, on Earth, though in the body of a small child. Herac spoke briefly with the child, though due to the constraints of the connection, and the age of the child, the responses were all terse, one-word answers. Herac found that Náftis was to be a healer, now in this new life-path. He was born into a family in central Europe with the means to make the dream possible for Náftis.

Herac also visited a person with whom he had had a lot of conflict in his worldly life. She had been living together with Herac closely for a time. Her name was Paraskínia. She had a debilitating disease which robbed her of her ability to move. In life, Herac was at a loss as to how to console Paraskínia. Herac had done the best he could to support her, though there were many triggers for the perpetual conflict between them.

When Herac saw Paraskínia, she had carried over the conflict to the ethereal realm. Herac then gave Paraskínia wings to afford her the freedom she had been robbed of in life. Paraskínia was ecstatic, and at once flew away in a joyful arc.

Nesting Dolls

We now have a divergence, and Herac's story takes perhaps a darker turn, in which ethereal beings are found who are hostile and in competition, as the drama between gods in Greek mythology so famously shows us.

*"Oh, baby, baby, it's a wild world
It's hard to get by just upon a smile"*

– Yusuf (Cat Stevens), "Wild World"

In the ethereal realm, one can meet brilliantly illumined beings, and also the extreme opposite, just as we can meet a wide range of temperaments in life below the summit. Any character, be it benevolent, or ferocious, or anything in between, can be encountered in this territory.

The difference in the etheric realm from our world is that the beings there are without bodies, and some of them crave a form when they see one. This desire can be trouble for those of us with open hearts – without protection, a loving and caring heart accepts all, even opportunistic and selfish beings. Removing these stowaways, or predators, and shielding from them can be problematic, to say the least. We must first be aware that such things are possible.

Just as a climber begins to doubt when nearing the thin air of the summit at Everest, we mere mortals are both in and out of our element. We have convinced ourselves that we are indeed not in our element at all. We are of the ether, all of us – this is the cloth from which we are cut.

If we just try to climb without acclimating, we might also increase our un-mindfulness, as the exponential increase in risk surges the higher we climb.

"The greatest danger for most of us is not that our aim is too high, and we miss it, but that it is too low, and we reach it."

– Michelangelo

Here, Herac struggles with vision problems and with the threat of a cancer recurrence.

And now we join Herac, feeling unsatisfied at the summit…

What Herac missed was engaging his mind to solve problems. That was what he had been born to do. Herac felt like a retired sleuth. Inactivity had rendered him useless. Herac felt his carefully honed mind slipping away more each day with disuse.

Herac thought about his health problems, his eyes and cancer – would he lose his sight entirely? Would the cancer within him return, waking from its dormancy?

Perhaps cancer was the opportunity for Herac to engage his mind and solve this great problem which plagued humanity. Herac was then rescued from worry over his eyes or cancer's return as other, more pressing issues came up...or down.

Herac suffered a spell of dizziness and collapsed after he had eaten his meal in the great hall of his home. Herac was incapacitated for a short time, then made a seemingly complete recovery. Others in the home thought they could notice some changes in Herac from the person they had known just the day before.

In the days and weeks following the lightheadedness, Herac also had an escalation in the number of visions that he had. Some visualizations were benign, others threatening. Herac being unable to use the remedy MT had suggested had affected his sight, and it had nearly completely begun to fail him. Reading, writing, and other activities which were so much a part of his life, these were now lost to Herac, and he missed the comfort they gave him.

In the void left by Herac's lost vision, he was compensated with enhanced visions born of the spirit realm, or mindscapes. These surrogate visions, in place of his sightless eyes, could be accurate, or – in most cases not at all.

The occupants of the spirit realm took notice of Herac's dependance on spirit-vision, and at once knew that Herac was as a child in the dark if not for the etheric mindscapes enhancing his vision.

At first, opportunistic spirits, comically playing jokes with Herac's vision, put objects in his path. Machines churned away in the center of his room, only to dissolve into the ether as Herac came close or walked through them. When faced with the ludicrous anomalies in his vision, Herac would sometimes bark orders and taunt the air, saying to the phantasms and the mischievous spirits who conjured them, "I know that's not there!" or, "Are you going to let me relieve my bladder?!" This snarky question was asked to an indifferent, churning set of gears as it blocked his path to the chamber pot. The brazen machineries happily ignored Herac and kept grinding away cheerfully. The phantasms would prevent Herac from eating and sleeping, and when he called out for help, there was often no answer from those nearby, and no escape from the rogue visions.

Ephemeral conjurings were the foreground in Herac's sight now, and he had to make peace with these new and troubling situations, dreams from which there was no waking.

Alternately captivating and inspiring visions would dance in Herac's mind like fireworks. Herac would also urgently want to share the inspiring visions he had, to stir and elevate the lives of those near him. These uplifting visions spoke in divine words and music, of healing, and love, of wonderous technology and magic. These were the visions Herac felt had come from God, now known to him as MT, who was soothing and caring for him.

The truly disturbing and dark visions, though, Herac did keep to himself, as he thought his giving voice to these phantasms would further invoke their presence, once again, to torment him.

During this time, loneliness and isolation also plagued Herac. Healers had managed to stabilize him to some degree, though his situation was precarious. The thread of his mind was stretched and fraying.

Friends and family offered Herac a brief and sweet solace from the specters, though many of those around him now had only the dimmest hint of how to connect with Herac, let alone give him comfort or aid in the quixotic crusades which he now felt such a resounding call to carry out, despite his waning frame. MT was a great comfort to Herac during this difficult time of recovery. MT would play soothing songs in his ear, and in his depression give him warm embraces. The songs Herac heard were of love, even romantic love, that also spoke to the profound and otherworldly love that a god such as MT could give. Herac felt cradled in love during this time, supported in every way, and soon he felt strong again, ready to step back into the world below the summit as he was required. Things went swimmingly for a long period and Herac was happy. He was given a break from any negative visions.

After a short time, suddenly he had a more aggressive resurgence in attacks of adverse images, mindscapes, and dreams. Herac felt these were personal attacks, and he thought they were messages from MT but were, shockingly, now malicious in nature. Herac was conflicted about these messages, which were supposed to have come from his creator. How could they possibly come from a being who held him as a mother holds a newborn?

Now, our tale diverges from an odd, but comfortable, spiritual reality, and becomes a Greek play, where drama is born…

Herac inquired of MT if he was behind the phantasmic assaults on him which had rattled him so badly. Herac asked MT, "Did *you* do this?"

"No. There is a god of our universe, Pesmenos. He is upset with our relationship. He's doing this to spite you!" Herac then discovered that MT operates in a hierarchy, where the god who created and maintains our universe, Pesmenos, is one apart from MT in ranking. Herac, before learning of Pesmenos, thought there was one God, and this God was responsible for all creation. Herac, with this knowledge of Pesmenos, now concluded there was a hierarchy, like nesting dolls, one within another.

The universes in which Pesmenos and MT presided were also nested one within another. Pesmenos' universe was exponentially of a different size than MT's. As MT and Herac's friendship had grown, Pesmenos, the god who created the universe, had become increasingly bitter. Pesmenos was jealous and fuming over Herac for MT's affection toward Herac – this new friend of Megalotypos, who had come uninvited to Pesmenos' domain. Pesmenos fumed, and began plotting against Herac, and when the time was ripe, Pesmenos pounced on Herac.

Herac was visiting his mother and sister in the spirit realm. They had both passed away and Herac longed to see them both.

MT had given Herac a spiritual estate in which to house his loved ones. Even the cat that Herac had loved in life was on the estate.

Pesmenos, in his smoldering rage, filled the sky of the estate with choking black soot. As the three were coughing and struggling to breathe, Herac called upon Megalotypos for help.

All that was missing from this assault on Herac and his family and cat were the flying monkeys from The Wizard of Oz…

Megalotypos took Pesmenos and, though he was his grandson, a legal celestial inquiry into to his actions was made.

Not only had Pesmenos attacked Herac and his loved ones, but Pesmenos, as creator of the universe, had failed to keep the universe safe from such dangers as the spread of the spawn of Cancer.

Cancer was more spider than crab. Her offspring went with her no matter where she traveled. The slender, lady-like legs, when nested in a host, would articulate with the flows of tumors within the victim, and ripe tissues would then transmute and form malicious, bastardized offspring, corrupting further the body, in silence. Enlisting cell after cell in unholy acts, until a majority ruled and the body was won, spirit in defeat, then abandoned. What once was its own, is now unrecognizable.

Cancer has overrun the population of Earth. The touch of Cancer entered through the nose of a sleeping victim at night, and the microscopic offspring of Cancer, tiny little crabs, would go up through the nose of the host to any type of organs in the body – lungs, brain, or eyes.

Pesmenos had allowed countless deaths, wars, and preventable disease to take place, and had taken no action to stop or slow these events.

A tribunal was called and weighed the evidence against Pesmenos to decide his fate. All Pesmenos' actions were recorded in the media of ether. The media of the ether itself recorded all events and could be played back by MT to see the events as they had happened so that no action or misdeed could ever illude the gods.

Meanwhile, Cancer had designs for Herac, and began to carry out these plans.

The great crab had begun to follow Herac. At dusk, with stealth, the arachnid let swarm tiny offspring into Herac's nose. As he breathed in, the spawn stole into Herac's body. The Cancers melded their slender legs, becoming one with the naked tissues of Herac's innermost and ungirded soft spots, the spawn gaining intimate bonds here and there, but most of all within Herac's seat of power. The toxic brood then lay dormant until the signal was given to stir new, hybrid flesh. The union of Cancer and Herac had begun. Herac had no inkling of awareness.

As the numbers of tiny Cancers increased within Herac, it weighed him down and caused him fatigue.

Herac then called on MT for help. MT banished Cancer's familiar and Herac was relieved not to see Cancer's minions pursuing him.

Because MT had healed him of Cancer's latest attack, Herac also thought that the infection of the brood of crabs inside him was gone, as well. However, this was not the case, and the colonies of Cancers still lay poised at strategic points inside Herac, waiting to strike if he showed disobedience to any future orders from the gods.

Upon a second infection and reactivation of the spawn of Cancer within him, Herac demanded of MT, "Did you not kill the Cancer spawn within me?!"

"No, it was only dormant." Herac was heartbroken upon learning this. While it had first been the actions of Pesmenos, then of MT himself, his Cancer had been given in the name of obedience. Herac could not believe that he had been betrayed by his creator.

Herac needed more information from MT about Cancer and so he asked, "If a newborn child is stricken by Cancer, why is it so?"

"Because the individual, born in a new being, had not obeyed in a prior lifetime."

Meanwhile, the tribunal had neared completion...The hearing found Pesmenos guilty, and sentenced him to spiritual death, though the death was not completely irrevocable, and at some point Pesmenos could possibly be called forth to life as a god in the future.

After the death of Pesmenos, Megalotypos was in a state of mourning and would not talk telepathically with

Herac. During the interval of MT's silence, Herac wanted to ensure the death of Cancer's spawn within him, and went to a trusted healer, Therapeftís, and this healer said to Herac, "You must say to yourself and the universe, 'I take back and fully embrace my power and I rest in this power that anchors me to the earth.'"

This mantra, repeated a small number of times, was enough to cure Herac of Cancer's resurgence.

After a long silence, MT began to share their wordless bond once again, and spoke with Herac.

MT also marveled at the healing of Herac, which had been evoked by the mantra. MT wanted Herac as the new creator and leader of the universe, to share the cure which had recently been so effective in defeating the malady spread by the brood of Cancer.

In the language of symbols, Megalotypos composed a script with the healing mantra Therapeftís had composed and evoked in Herac. This could then be shared in dreams and meditations throughout the earth and the universe in innumerable beings affected by the spawn of Cancer.

Time had passed since the demise of Pesmenos. The position of god-in-charge of the universe had been vacated. The position was offered to Herac by MT. Herac was shown a throne with his name engraved on a brass plate, to his utter amazement.

Herac was then walking through a mindscape. Since his vision was still impaired, he often would do this. In the mindscape, he came upon a mound with a shield on top. This was the new resting place of Pesmenos after his passing.

As Herac drew close to the shield, up sprang Pesmenos, blade in hand, in a ravenous attack.

"Aaaaaaahhh!" Pesmenos yelled as he lunged.

Herac fell backward. In utter shock, he recoiled and drew his arms up defensively.

Underneath the shield was the hidden passage from which Pesmenos had leapt, swiping at Herac with a large sword.

Herac was, of course, taken aback. His heart leapt in his chest, though he was able to dodge the blows and escape Pesmenos' attack.

Herac began calling out to MT in his mind, pleading, once again, for help.

Then the violent, yet ephemeral, scene vanished. Herac was alone at the mound, catching his breath, and fuming.

Herac was, of course, livid with MT, because he had been assured that Pesmenos had been put to spiritual death and was not a problem.

Pesmenos was again subject to a tribunal and was again punished, not to return to act in vengeance on Herac or others. Perhaps the love of MT toward Pesmenos had allowed him to return from spiritual death and seek retaliation on Herac. Herac doubted MT and thought that he was lying when he said that Pesmenos had been put to spiritual death.

MT was, at the same moment, irate with Herac. When the time had come for him to trust MT, to trust that Pesmenos was, in fact, dead, a complete lack of faith was shown. Herac had, this time, failed and lost faith that MT had, in fact, kept his word.

The scene with Pesmenos had been an elaborate test, to determine Herac's depth of loyalty to and love and devotion for MT, and Herac had failed miserably.

Punishment descended on Herac for his doubt of MT. Phantasmic visions tormented Herac, and he was lost in the onslaught, left in a crumpled heap on the ground, bleeding.

Herac, with some help from healers, recovered from the tempestuous upheaval of his world and pleaded for mercy from MT.

Herac promised his obedience to MT, calm was restored, and he also resumed his friendly, wordless chats with Herac… It was as if nothing had happened.

From these events, we can see that the gods of the ether are those of Greek dramas. I feel the spirits encountered in the beginning of our tale were much closer to our one, omnipotent God. As corruption from harmful entities took its toll, the ether and its beings, in Herac's eyes, were swept up in and corrupted by intense drama. This drama, drawn from Herac's own tethers to and from below the summit, our mundane world… Herac was now a man in two worlds simultaneously… He drew up negativity from below, and was drawn to commotion in the ether…

Our kite had been fouled in mud, and the muck had clung on, bringing the mire to heaven, paradise lost in the befoulment, at least for a time.

Herac had three recurrences of the waxing and waning Cancer spawn within him, and the third time, Herac asked MT, "Is it you who's responsible for the reawakening of the brood within me?"

"It was me," MT replied.

"Why would you do that?!"

"To ensure obedience." Herac was, of course, taken aback by this admission, though he was grateful for the third and final healing of his Cancer. Herac understood that MT needed him to be obedient if he was to be of service in the ethereal realm. There was no more talk of the issue between MT and Herac. The matter latterly passed – though the sting and anxiety caused by MT's seemingly icy, reptilian actions echoed in Herac's memory.

Then MT lit a candle in Herac's darkness... Megalotypos told Herac that there were 100 universes beyond the one in which he lived, and that MT himself had laid the groundwork for communication between these universes. It would take Herac at least an entire lifetime to travel from one to another, even at the speed of light. MT, in traveling himself from universe to universe, extended his own nervous system, so that instantaneous communication was possible from one world to another. Herac wanted to visit an alternative universe and asked Megalotypos to allow him to see the closest one, which was merely one of Herac's lifetimes away, travelling at the speed of light. Herac was given a ship and crew.

Upon arrival at the new world, Herac placed his engineer on the ground to try to steer the ship through the steep spires of a canyon. The scout was captured and tortured by the aboriginal people of the planet. His eyes were cut out.

After this hostile gesture of welcome by the king of planet Makria, Herac and his crew were given an opportunity to negotiate and speak with the king's entourage.

A stipulation of the meeting was that Herac, and his attending crew were to surrender a body part. This would be kept in stasis and returned to Herac and his crew, after an audience with the king's court.

Herac refused to negotiate with such an obvious disadvantage and stormed the castle. The crew used their energy weapons to stun the barbarians. The king of the planet was also subdued, and the battle was short-lived due to Herac and his crew's superior weaponry.

After the battle, Herac was pensive. It had been almost too easy to defeat the king and his guards. Herac and his crew's liberation of the castle was a success!

He and the crew went to inspect the spoils of their victory, and to see what else they could find within the depths of the castle. Herac thought he may find more guards holding out inside.

After a long and most fruitless search, Herac reached the queen's chamber. She cried, "You arrived at the perfect time… Our King is insane and wants nothing but to dominate those who oppose him!" He holds the body parts of those who speak out against him." She showed Herac beneath the visor of her headpiece, and one of her eyes was missing.

Herac took pity on the queen. "You can come back with us to our world, which is more peaceful."

Herac asked the queen if there was any possibility to talk with the king when he recovered from the effects

ALLEN and DAVID GLINIEWICZ

of the energy weapons Herac and the crew used to subdue him and his men.

"Only through the surrender of your most precious body part," the queen said. She gestured to her hips and her eyes dragged the floor, avoiding Herac's. "I can bring you to where those who want an audience with the king wait."

Herac had used a lift to get to the upper floors during his search. However, the lower floors had restricted access.

Herac went to the lift, assuming that was how to get to the lower floors.

"No, we will walk down," the queen said.

Herac thought it odd, but followed wordlessly as the queen strode down the spiral stairs.

They descended to where the men were kept. As they treaded downward, the queen matter-of-factly gestured to the lighted panels built into the wall of the stairwell.

Hands, feet, blue and green eyes with nerves twitching, phalluses, breasts, kidneys, lungs quivering and billowing, all tastefully backlit in laser-contained stasis pods, graced the walls as they strode down.

The queen said casually, "Oh, he likes to see that his visitors are healthy on the way to negotiations, every part of them."

Herac didn't look at the queen, but he could hear the stifled smirk in her voice as she held back from spitting her words. She covered her distain with an oily quietude.

Herac's stomach sank, and he knew there was no

hope of finding any common ground with the king. He was truly and violently deranged.

Herac felt he had to try to free the prisoners down below, but not without all their necessary anatomy.

Herac then said to the queen, "We should just go, as soon as we can, but not before rescuing my engineer! You can come with me. Why don't we get your eye? Show me where it is." The queen agreed. They retrieved her emerald-colored eye from the king's chamber. They then went to find the engineer. He was in a heap on the floor of a cell, and had been defaced, quite literally. He was missing his eyes and had severe wounds in his chest, and most of his liver was gone.

The queen located the body segments the engineer was missing.

Herac needed to carry the engineer, along with his fleshly trimmings.

Herac and the queen took the engineer and other unfortunate appointment-holders with the king, and their anatomic keepsakes, back to the ship.

Herac was ready to leave the planet with the queen, as he had promised.

After helping the engineer and prisoners to the recovery room, the queen disappeared, along with her green eye. She neglected to have her eye socket reunited with its counterpart in the medical bay of the ship.

Seemingly of its own accord, the ship spun abruptly from its hover, then began flying toward the castle's battlements.

Shocked, Herac knew the ship would never move without him. Only on *his* orders would it do this.

And it sure as hell would not be hurtling about chaotically on a collision course. Herac went to find who was responsible, though he had a good idea who it might be. There was only one place where the remote control could be happening – an emergency station in the lower decks from which, if the bridge was compromised, the ship could be flown.

The queen had overpowered and mutilated an officer to gain access to the ship's controls, the officer lay in what looked more like a collection of parts than a person, lay on the ship's deck. The queen's latest victim, who had been stationed at the emergency remote panel now, like the queen, was missing an eye. It had been completely ripped out forcefully. A red-and-white smear was on the floor near the officer – a gelatinous puddle of clear and white, with hints of blue and hazel. Clearly this was what once was the officer Helena's eye.

Herac went to the emergency station. He saw the massacred body of Helena and subdued the queen with his energy weapon.

The queen was returned to the surface while still unconscious, and the ship then left.

Breathing heavily, Herac felt such relief that they had left the queen and Makria behind.

He turned to head back to recovery and noticed the queen's green eye in the stasis pad on the floor near the transport pad. "She must have put it down to pilot the ship!" Herac laughed, "An eye for an eye!"

He sent the now-conscious injured officer to the infirmary with the queen's forgotten eye. Herac, his crew, and their ship returned to their own universe, grateful to be back in their safe, yet flawed world. Herac also knew that it was not so imperfect as compared to where he had just been. Herac reflected on the differences between his world and that of Makria.

He tried to forget the terrors and the savagery. Herac shuddered… and thanked God he was home!

Herac had another afterthought… *Did the king and queen go browsing for parts like window-shopping for clothes?*

The contents of his stomach suddenly wanted to retrace the path to his mouth. Herac was now even more glad to be free from Makria. Part of him, though, would never be free…

Another, darker thought crept into the recesses of Herac's mind. Had MT shown Makria to him because there were parts of the ether that were just as dangerous and brutal? Herac then understood why Megalotypos had allowed him to see the other universe. Herac saw that it was no better than his own and had the same struggles. The inhabitants had made their own choices and had developed into what they thought was an ideal society. However, things like trust and love were notably absent from Makria.

The absence of these crucial ingredients, love and caring, had created a world based on fear, competition, and bloodlust. It was as if the ancient Romans – with perhaps a bit of Machiavelli thrown in – with blood sport and spectacle, gladiator battles, and treachery, had been the ruling caste of Makria. Makria, a planet devoid of love.

Herac felt MT had taught him a lesson. In having experienced a world so devoid of compassion, empathy, and caring, Herac began to see the value of love, and trust, and – perhaps most of all – self-love. Herac had experienced the smallest part of self-love, and it began to dawn on him that it was the seed from which any love is born.

A bright spot in the conflict and drama of Herac's adventures… And a new level of nesting is about to be revealed…

Simultaneously, during Herac's travels and experiences, he contacted a being called The Little Luminous Boy, also known as Tapihritsa or Tapi. He was a seventh-century Tibetan master who acquired a radiant "light" body and was such an illuminated master that from the age of three he was instrumental in developing the Bon religion in Tibet, the precursor to Tibetan Buddhism. Until the age of nine, Tapi would practice meditation four to five hours per day and attend lectures with the Bon masters. Tapi was instrumental in formalizing the four tenets of the Bon spiritual path and disseminating it to the population of the country. Tapi passed away while meditating in the snow outside of his Himalayan cave at age forty.

Herac, through telepathy, was able to contact and interview Tapi and have it recorded in the ethereal media, as it had been in Pesmenos' tribunals.

The incarnation of Tapi to whom Herac later spoke, in a deep telepathic contact, had lived from 1840 to 1860, reaching the age of twenty years. This reincarnation was one of the first casualties in the Civil War in the United

States. Herac was able to contact and speak with this last incarnation of Tapi, who had lived in Booneville, Tennessee.

Herac and Tapihritsa became close, and there was a bond which perhaps surpassed the relationship between Herac and MT. Herac and Tapi became counselors to the god under MT's direction, and life was good for a few weeks.

After all these adventures and intrigues with MT and Pesmenos, Herac heard a deep, authoritative voice in his meditation. This new voice belonged to a god above MT, who presided over a universe described as exponentially larger than that of MT.

Herac called the new god Apeiro. This god disciplined Herac as MT had done, and even to a further degree, and Herac knew that Apeiro was serious, and that he'd better fall in line.

Herac marveled at the impossibly large distances in the immense universe over which Apeiro presided. And he said a fond farewell to MT, knowing that he now had moved up to the next level in the nesting universes. Herac and MT parted on the best of terms, though Herac felt some loss during their goodbye.

Apeiro had decided, after some back-and-forth with Herac and Tapi, that they would be counsellors for Apeiro – a group of trusted advisors. The issues sprang from Herac and Tapi's close relationship. Apeiro thought it could possibly cloud Herac and Tapi's judgment in matters of responsibility. Herac stood up for Tapi, and Apeiro reconsidered.

Herac's former post – as the caretaker for the

universe in which we live – was to be given to Herac's mother, Alíki. She was being trained for this new role.

And so, it would seem to be the end of the tale of Herac, now a counselor to Apeiro with his dear friend Tapi.

"Curiouser and curiouser!"

– Lewis Carroll, *Alice in Wonderland*

David

You may ask, is Apeiro who he claims to be, a god above all others?

Herac was not too surprised to hear Apeiro admit that, like all the gods prior, there is another presiding above him, another nesting level.

And so, the nesting continues, each one giving to another, Herac endlessly fascinated in sleuthing out the sources and trappings of each new level.

Entities of the ether do extend their influence on the mundane world and in the ephemeral, as they have in Herac's case, and perhaps gain access to his formidable mind.

One thing that sticks out – for all the gods Herac has met, none of them offered a name for themselves! All the names given to the gods have been applied by Herac. This raises a question as to the true identities of the gods. Do the gods have identities and roles prior to Herac bestowing a name? Is an entity in the ether formless until Herac gives them a form and a role? These questions are indeed mysteries that give us something to think about, for sure.

I did warn you this was a cautionary tale... Is Herac the boy who climbed the glass mountain, now lying beside the dead golden knight, waiting for the eagle to carry him skyward?

Herac's story is still unfolding, and perhaps with the one true God's help and protection, Herac and a god without nicknames will prevail and reach the summit. Perhaps Herac is much more of a sherpa now, who has met the single greatest challenge of his life, in any world. Time will tell us where Herac is and where he's going…

And now, back in the mundane world…

Let me say that it's been a wild ride with Allen. He did attain the physical summit of the glass mountain in our mundane world! Though, the ethereal realm is a much more entangled jungle, unfortunately. Like I said before, we must be discriminating as to what entities we may meet in the world of spirit, and what status we give to them, and what boundaries we keep with spirits.

Best to all of us in our own climbs. God is the guide to the sherpa. Let's be one of them, rather than a DaVinci, who surely could not deal with the likes of Apeiro and Pesmenos. No tanks nor flying machines are going to make a difference in the ether. No magic or tech is going to save us in that nebulous and indefinable place.

Vaya con Dios!

"An aged man is but a paltry thing,
A tattered coat upon a stick, unless
Soul clap its hands and sing, and louder sing
For every tatter in its mortal dress..."

– William Butler Yeats, "Sailing to Byzantium"

Allen and David

Epilogue

Allen and I thank you for your indulgence for our many strains of credulity throughout our time together.

My dad, as a parting sentiment, wanted to share that when approaching entities, one does need discernment and to approach with a positive mind. The posture of one's approach is everything.

I feel this quote offers some help to each of us that must walk a path as we age…

"Die in the morning so you need not die at night."

– Ram Dass, Conscious Aging

What Ram Dass means is if we have a spiritual practice and center, and if we find out who we actually are and what we are doing on the planet, we won't get swept up in drama when we are old and closer to the ends of our lives.

The blazing alarm bells of our bodies' ailments can't rattle us if we have the inner resonance and solidity that can keep us grounded in the face of any trial, even hostile spirits! I don't know if I'm ready for a challenge like Allen is in the thick of having. I don't know if any of us are.

I do know that most of all we need devotion and love, and most of all *self*-love. These are the pillars of being human. A handy acronym taught to me by Joseph Carbone, my mentor and healer, is KLUF. Be these things, always – Kind, Loving, Understanding, and Forgiving.

Personally, I feel a sherpa's spirit accompanies me on this journey with Allen. I feel as though devotion may have gone a long way in preventing a Greek drama from spilling into these pages.

God Bless!
~ Allen and Me ~

Thank you for embarking on this incredible journey with Al and me.

If you found joy in the first installment of Climbing the Glass Mountain, I'd be honored if you could take a moment to share your experience through an Amazon review. Your words can be a guiding light for other readers, nudging them to explore the world we've created together. I'm eager to hear your thoughts—what resonated with you, or any insights you may have. Your feedback means the world to both Allen and me. Your review is not just a reflection of our journey; it's a shared celebration. Thank you for being a part of this literary adventure!

Review link - https://mybook.to/CTGMGliniewicz

Exciting News! The adventure doesn't end here – our book is now part of the eagerly anticipated Ethereal Labyrinth Series. Brace yourselves because a thrilling sequel is already in the works, set to captivate you by early 2025. Prepare to dive deeper into the mythical territory teased at the end of Volume 1. We're taking you farther down the rabbit hole, unlocking new dimensions of wonder and mystery. Stay tuned for an even more enchanting journey in the next chapter of Climbing the Glass Mountain!

Best and blessings,

David Gliniewicz
San Francisco, Bay Area
Email: contact@davidauthor.com

David Gliniewicz is a multifaceted individual with a deep passion for the paranormal, spiritual exploration, and technology. Before embarking on his journey as a storyteller, he navigated diverse professional roles, including being a radiologic technologist, a proficient musician, a computer enthusiast, and a respected professor in the diagnostic medical imaging program at City College of San Francisco.

The rhythmic allure of music has always been a driving force in David's life, whether through chanting, playing instruments, or singing. This profound connection to music permeates his creative projects, infusing them with a unique and inspiring energy.

Beyond his professional and artistic pursuits, David aspires to bridge the gap between the spiritual realm and our everyday lives. This vision is exemplified in his storytelling, with Allen's narrative serving as a testament to this desire. David's future endeavors promise to delve even deeper into the exploration of spiritual dimensions, offering readers a captivating and enlightening journey.

Connect with David:

Amazon Author Page
https://www.amazon.com/author/david.glin

Tiktok
https://www.tiktok.com/@davidgliniewicz38

Patreon
https://www.patreon.com/ClimbingtheGlassMountain

Facebook
David Gliniewicz Author

Reddit
https://www.reddit.com/u/MeringueHot9981/s/NhwM ho5zNw

YouTube
https://youtube.com/@DavidGliniewicz.Author

WordPress
http://climbingtheglassmountain.com
https://davidauthor.com/
http://etherreadsemporium.com

Made in United States
Troutdale, OR
07/16/2024

21258574R00100